THE WESTMINSTER CONFESSION FOR TODAY

the
WESTMINSTER CONFESSION
for today

---

a contemporary interpretation
by George S. Hendry

JOHN KNOX PRESS
RICHMOND, VIRGINIA

Library of Congress Catalog Card Number: 60-6283

© C. D. Deans 1960
Printed in the United States of America
6737

■ contents

Contents 7

■ introduction

The Christian church has since early times drawn up statements of its faith, either in the form of brief summaries of the principal "articles" or elements in it, such as the Apostles' Creed, or in the form of more detailed and elaborate documents, like the Westminster Confession of Faith. These statements have been designed to serve various purposes. The Apostles' Creed, which probably developed from the creed recited by converts at their baptism in the ancient Roman Church, is suitable for recitation by Christians as a way of testifying to their faith; it names the chief elements involved in Christian faith, without any interpretation or explanation. Others, such as the Nicene Creed, were drawn up for the purpose of providing authoritative guidance in the interpretation of specific articles of faith about which dispute had arisen; they were intended to present "the right view" (this is the literal meaning of ortho-doxy) of the article in question. Later, at the Reformation, when the area of dispute grew so wide that Christendom was rent asunder, it became the custom for the Protestant Churches to draw up confessions which were intended to present the right view of all the articles of the faith; to this group belongs the Confession of Faith, which is held by the Presbyterian Churches as their principal "standard."

The Confession of Faith was drawn up by an assembly of divines which was summoned at Westminster in 1643 by the English Parliament in order to prepare a scheme for uniformity of religion in the recently united kingdom of England and Scotland. In addition to the Confession of Faith, which it completed on November 26, 1646, the Assembly also produced the Form of Church Government, the Directory for Public Worship, and the Larger and Shorter Catechisms. The scheme for a unified Presbyterian Church in both parts of the United Kingdom was defeated by the re-establishment of episcopacy in England at the restoration of the Stuart monarchy in 1661. The Confession, however, had in the meantime been adopted by the General Assembly of the Church of Scotland in 1649, and it has continued to be recognized as the principal "subordinate standard" of that Church to the present day. It also found favor, along with the Catechisms, among the Presbyterians of England and Ireland. It was brought to America by early settlers, and was adopted by the General Synod of the Presbyterian Church in 1729 as "the confession of their faith," with the exception of certain clauses relating to the civil magistrate. Similarly it was adopted by the United Presbyterian Church at its formation in 1728, and by the Presbyterian Church in the United States in 1861. It is surely one of the ironies of history that Presbyterian Churches throughout the English-speaking world should hold as their standards a group of documents which were almost entirely the work of episcopally ordained clergymen of the Church of England.

The Confession of Faith was not intended to serve as a text for instruction in the Christian faith. This was the function which its authors had in mind for the two Catechisms which accompanied it.[1] But since the Catechisms have largely fallen into disuse (and the catechetical method into disfavor among educators), the function has tended to devolve on the Confession. The number of commentaries and expositions of it that have appeared within the last hundred years is a witness to the increasing role it has come to play as a manual of instruction in the faith.

---

[1] It is said to have been the belief of the Westminster divines that the Larger Catechism would be the most extensively used of all their productions; it has, in fact, been the least.

II

The propriety of using the Confession as the basis of an exposition of the church's faith at the present day, however, raises a number of questions which demand further consideration. The fact cannot be ignored that the Confession no longer holds the same place in the mind of the church as it did in the past. While most Presbyterian Churches on both sides of the Atlantic continue formally to accept the Confession, they do so with certain expressed and unexpressed qualifications and reservations. Some have introduced changes in the text of the Confession itself, by altering certain passages, by eliminating others, and by adding new chapters. Some have taken formal action to define the sense in which they interpret certain passages or to preclude certain inferences that might be drawn from them. Several Churches have adopted brief statements of faith, which, while "they are not to be regarded as substitutes for, but rather as interpretations of, and supplements to, the Westminster Confession,"[2] do in fact constitute implicit revisions of it. Individual members of the Churches have called for a thorough revision of the Confession, and some have proposed the preparation of an entirely new Confession which would in effect supersede the old, but no Presbyterian Church has thus far committed itself to such a step.

The attitude of the Presbyterian Churches toward their Confession of Faith, which they accept and at the same time criticize, may appear to be anomalous, but it is in accordance with the Confession itself. For the central principle of the Reformed faith, which it asserts, is that the Word of God is the only infallible rule of faith and practice, and that no other document—not even one produced under the best ecclesiastical auspices—can be regarded in the same light. One of the main reasons why the Re-

---

[2] From the (abortive) Plan of Union between the Presbyterian Church in the USA, the Presbyterian Church in the US, and the United Presbyterian Church of North America, 1954, p. 261. The same language is used in the Plan of Union between the first and last named of these Churches, which was consummated in 1958.

formers were constrained to break with the Roman Church was that their doctrines, which were the products of the mind of the church, were propounded as "dogmas divinely revealed" and therefore "infallible and irreformable." The Confession of Faith affirms explicitly and emphatically that "all decrees of councils" and "doctrines of men" are subject to the judgment of "the Supreme Judge," who "can be no other but the Holy Spirit speaking in the Scripture" (CF I, 10), and are therefore open to correction; and in saying this it does not intend to exempt itself, for it also states that "All synods or councils since the apostles' times, whether general or particular [and the Westminster Assembly comes under this category], may err" (CF XXXIII, 3). Immunity from criticism is the last thing its authors would claim for the Confession. Their main endeavor is to refer us to the Word of God; if continued study of the Word of God (and it has been under continuous study in the church during the three centuries that have elapsed since the Confession was drawn up) leads us to take exception to some statements in the Confession, this is not to show disrespect for it; on the contrary, it is to treat it with the highest degree of respect.

This, of course, does not answer the practical question of how acceptance of the Confession of Faith can be combined with exception to some of its statements, or how the line between acceptance and exception is to be drawn. To this question various answers have been offered. One is suggested in the formula of subscription required of ministers in the United Presbyterian Church in the USA, who are asked whether they accept the Confession of Faith "as containing the system of doctrine taught in the Holy Scriptures"; it has been held that acceptance of the *system* does not imply acceptance of every individual doctrine in it. But it would be difficult to say precisely how the distinction between the system and the doctrines is to be drawn, and perhaps this is only a restatement of the problem rather than a solution to it. A similar distinction is indicated in the ordination formula of the Church of Scotland, which requires acceptance of "the fundamental doctrines of the Christian faith contained in the Confession of Faith of this Church," and it is explained that this is compatible with "recognising liberty of opinion on such points of doctrine as do not enter into the substance of the faith." It may be granted that the distinction suggested here is workable up to a point, but difficulty is likely to arise when there is difference of opinion as to whether a specific point of doctrine does or does not "enter into the substance of the faith"—or as to what precisely this phrase means.

Both of these formulas suggest some kind of distinction within the area of doctrine itself, between some doctrines and others; and this may serve the purpose to some extent. But it is inadequate, and may even be dangerously misleading, as may be shown by a simple example. There are undoubtedly some doctrines which so "enter into the substance of the faith" that rejection of them would seem to be equivalent to repudiation of the faith. Thus, acceptance of the doctrine that God exists would seem to be an indispensable requirement for any faith at all—"for he that cometh to God must believe that he is." (Heb. 11:6.) Yet the two things do not necessarily coincide. There is a difference between believing in God "at the top of your mind" and believing in God "at the bottom of your heart," as John Baillie has aptly put it. According to the psalmist, the real "atheist" is the man who says *in his heart,* There is no God (Ps. 14:1), and according to Christ, such a man may be found among those who are loudest in their vocal protestations of belief (Matt. 7:21-23). It seems clear that there is a distinction we have to recognize between all doctrines as such, and the faith with which they are concerned. Of course they are very closely and intimately related; a confession of faith can only take the form of a statement of doctrines. Yet doctrines are not faith; they are statements of faith in propositional form.

Faith has often been compared to a journey, or a pilgrimage. Doctrine may then be compared to a map. No one would suppose he had reached his destination merely because he had located it on the map, or traced the route that leads to it. Yet the map is an indispensable aid to any traveler in unfamiliar country. And just as the map is right when it enables the traveler to reach the end of his journey, so doctrine is right when it enables the pilgrim to reach "the end of his faith." (See I Peter 1:9.) Like the traveler himself, it is justified by faith. But it is never "infallible and irreformable." Although the main features of the landscape remain unchanged from age to age and will appear on every map, building and road developments and improvements in the art of cartography call constantly for the production of new maps to assist the traveler to make the journey under the conditions which exist in his own day—and not under those which existed at the time of his father or his grandfather. If it is true that "New occasions teach new duties; Time makes ancient good uncouth,"[3] new insights derived from faithful study of the Word of God, and new conditions under which the journey of faith has to be made, require that the maps of doctrine, which did good service to our forefathers in their journey, must be revised and amended if they are to fulfill that service for us.

III

The Confession of Faith possesses great and undoubted merits. It could not have held its place in the Presbyterian Churches for so long if that were not so. The time and care devoted to its preparation, the systematic skill with which it handles the whole field of doctrine, the courage with which it faces the most difficult questions, the precision, elegance, and occasional nobility of the language it uses, combine to make it, in its way, a minor classic. But a classic suggests an old work, and the chief fault of the Confession, if it is a fault, is simply that it is old. The Confession was a product of the seventeenth century, and it exhibits a number of features which are characteristic of the temper and mentality of that period but which are less congenial to the mind of the church at the present day. Four of these may be indicated briefly:

1. The manner of approach is excessively legalistic. This was characteristic of the period, which was preoccupied with consti-

---

[3] From "The Present Crisis" by James Russell Lowell.

tutional questions, and the specific circumstances under which the Confession originated made it almost inescapable. The main business of the Westminster Assembly of divines was to prepare a form of church government, and it was to this that they put their hand first. Matters of doctrine were not in serious dispute, and the preparation of a confession was conceived as part of the larger project. The Confession therefore has more of the character of a constitutional than a confessional document. This is reflected in the style; with its precise phrasing, its cumbrous involutions and repetitions, the multiplication of prepositions and qualifying clauses, it often sounds like a legal contract. It is a question whether this kind of language (and the mentality that goes with it) is the best medium for the presentation of the doctrine of the gospel.

2. The authors of the Confession, in common with most of the men of their age, thought it was incumbent upon them to deliver categorical answers to all questions that could be raised concerning the faith, and not only so, but they held the attitude that to every question there is one right answer, and all the others are wrong. They seem to have forgotten that "we walk by faith, not by sight" (II Cor. 5:7), and "we see through a glass, darkly" (I Cor. 13:12). Only once do they hint at mystery (CF III, 8); for the rest, they know all the answers, and can explain everything. This is particularly evident in the two final chapters, in which the Confession takes us, so to speak, on a conducted tour of the shadowy region beyond death, and not only does it know how to distinguish the stages of the journey we shall have to take there, but it predicts the issue of the final judgment with a confidence hardly befitting those who will be neither judge nor jury, but judged.

3. The Confession tends to see everything in terms of black and white; there are no intermediate shades of gray. The gospel is construed in the framework of a gigantic drama, which begins when God in his eternal decree separates the elect from the reprobate (CF III), and ends at the last judgment when he separates the righteous from the wicked for all eternity; and at every

stage of the drama, as it unfolds, the Confession seeks the motif in the separation that is going on beneath the surface (where they are mixed up together) between the good and the bad, the sheep and the goats, the wheat and the tares. The Confession struggles valiantly to trace the line that divides them; but there are some difficult borderline cases—elect persons who never get to hear the word (CF XII, 3), good people who do not profess the Christian religion (CF XII, 4), unregenerate men who do good acts (CF XVIII, 7)—and with these the line takes such twists and turns that it becomes impossible to follow it. Is this kind of segregation-ism a matter of concern to faith?

4. The Confession tends to view the drama of redemption as one that is played out between God and the individual. The social aspect of the drama is formally recognized—in the doc-trines of the covenant (CF VII), the church (CF XXVII), and the communion of saints (CF XXVIII)—but its significance is not fully realized and it is not integrated into the picture as a whole. It is the individual who occupies the stage for most of the time; rarely do we catch a glimpse of his "neighbor"—this Biblical word is absent from the Confession. Even marriage is described much like a business partnership between two individuals, and love is not so much as mentioned.[4]

Should any reader interpret these observations as a plea to the church to consider whether the time has not come to trade in the Confession for a new one, the writer would not take serious ex-ception. He would point out, however, that until a new and bet-ter Confession is forthcoming, we must continue to use the old one, with such adjustments and repairs as may be necessary to keep it in a roadworthy condition. The present commentary has been written in the belief that the Confession of Faith, if it is treated with care and discrimination, can still render valuable service to the traveler on the road of faith.

---

[4] The above sentence was written with reference to Chapter XXVI in its original form. It is less applicable to the revised chapter of 1959—yet here, too, the final clause still applies!

EXPLANATION OF ABBREVIATIONS

CF The Confession of Faith. Chapters are cited in Roman numerals, and paragraphs in Arabic. Thus CF XXVII, 3 refers to the Confession of Faith, chapter twenty-seven, paragraph three.

LC The Larger Catechism.

SC The Shorter Catechism.

▪ chapter I

OF THE HOLY SCRIPTURE

The first question which may properly be asked of anyone who claims to have knowledge is, How do you know? The Christian church, in confessing its faith, claims to have access to a certain knowledge concerning the ultimate mystery in which we are involved; and since this could not be classified as "common knowledge," the church must be prepared to answer the question, when it is asked, How did you come by this knowledge? Indeed, ✔ the church must ask the question itself, for the clarification of its own mind regarding the faith it confesses.

The first chapter of the Confession is devoted to answering this question. The source of the knowledge possessed by the Christian church is the Bible:

> "Jesus loves me! this I know,
> For the Bible tells me so."

The answer is easily given. But as the length of the chapter indicates (it is one of the longest in the Confession), the Bible itself requires a good deal of explanation if we are to be able to understand it and use it aright. For the Bible is not an easy book, and there are many questions we want to ask about it: What kind of book is it? What is it all about? How did it come to be written? How do the various parts of it hang together? How did it come to hold the place it does in the Christian church? How are we to use it so that it will serve the purpose it was intended to serve? It is with questions like these about the Bible that the Confession deals in this chapter.

CF I,1   Although the light of nature, and the works of
creation and providence, do so far manifest the goodness, wisdom, and power of God, as to leave men inexcusable; yet are they not sufficient to give that
knowledge of God, and of his will, which is necessary
unto salvation; therefore it pleased the Lord, at sundry
times, and in divers manners, to reveal himself, and to
declare that his will unto his church; and afterwards
for the better preserving and propagating of the truth,
and for the more sure establishment and comfort of
the church against the corruption of the flesh, and the
malice of Satan and of the world, to commit the same
wholly unto writing; which maketh the Holy Scripture to be most necessary; those former ways of God's
revealing his will unto his people being now ceased.

The natural question to ask first about the Bible, as of any
book which comes into our hands, is, What is it about? It is not
a question that can always be answered informatively in a single
word or phrase. Some books are about many things; and on the
face of it, the Bible is a book of very varied contents. Indeed, it
has often been said that the Bible is not a book but a library of
books. This has made it difficult for readers to find the answer to
the question, What is the Bible about? because they have been
bewildered by its variegated contents and unable, as it were, to
see the forest for the trees. This was the problem of the Ethiopian
eunuch, as he sat in his chariot reading a portion of the Old
Testament, until Philip came to his aid and told him "what it
was all about." (Acts 8:26-40.) In like manner the Confession
comes to our aid and offers us a clue to guide us in our reading
of the Bible; it tells us that the Bible is about:

"that knowledge of God, and of his will, which is necessary
unto salvation." There are three things which it is important to
notice about this description of the theme of the Bible: (1) It is
knowledge of God the Bible is concerned with. This does not
mean that knowledge of other subjects may not be involved as

well; but the Confession makes it clear that knowledge of God is the principal subject. (2) It is knowledge of God's will. It is a practical rather than a theoretical kind of knowledge. It is not a knowledge that serves merely to satisfy our intellectual curiosity or to fill up gaps in our understanding; it is a knowledge which obliges us to decide and act. (3) It is necessary to salvation. It is a matter of life and death to us. It is not merely knowledge of a way in which we may choose to act; it confronts us with a decision on which the ultimate issues of our life depend.

2.

3.

This knowledge is the theme of the Bible. But the Bible is not itself the source of it. The Confession looks behind the Bible to the ultimate source of the saving knowledge of God in revelation.

"it pleased the Lord . . . to reveal himself." To "re-veal" means simply to "un-veil," to remove a veil and expose to view some person or object that was previously concealed behind it. When the Confession speaks of God revealing himself, it implies that apart from his revelation of himself God is hidden and unknown. Does this mean that God is completely hidden and that we can know nothing about him at all except through the revelation to which the Bible gives us access? This is the question to which the opening clause of the paragraph refers.

"the light of nature, and the works of creation and providence, do so far manifest the goodness, wisdom, and power of God, as to leave men inexcusable." The Confession seems here to affirm a partial or potential knowledge of God (or, perhaps, knowledge *about* God) which is available to men through evidence of certain of his attributes in the world around us and which the human mind is capable of grasping in virtue of its natural endowment ("the light of nature"). This conception is often called natural revelation, or general revelation (to distinguish it from the special revelation to which the Bible gives access), but the name is misleading, since it is really thought of as a knowledge of God which is available without revelation at all. The idea of such a general revelation was first formulated by some of the philosophers of ancient Greece, and it was readily welcomed, for the most part, by the theologians of the early church, who saw in it a useful

point of contact for the message of the special or Christian revelation, just as Paul in his speech at Athens had cited a knowledge
of God to which pagan worship and pagan thought bore witness,
and had used it as a peg on which to hang the message of God in
Christ. It came to be more or less the established view of the
church that a certain knowledge of God, comprising at least a
knowledge of his existence and some of his attributes, is accessible
to all rational beings by general revelation and forms the foundation or presupposition of the saving knowledge of God which is
given by special revelation. This is the official teaching of the
Roman Catholic Church, and it has been widely accepted by
Protestants as well. But not by all; and in recent times it has been
vigorously contested by some, who have taken the position that
the faith of the Christian church is bound exclusively to the
special revelation and that there can be no place in it for the
idea of a general revelation or natural knowledge of God. It is
instructive to glance briefly at some of the more important issues
that have been raised in the discussion of this difficult problem.

(1) Belief in God is widespread beyond the limits of those who
have received special revelation, and there seems to be no other
way of accounting for it than by the idea of general revelation.
There have been times when belief in God was (or was thought
to be) virtually universal; and this has led some to think that a
certain knowledge of God was innate in the human mind. The
prevalence of unbelief in the modern world has altered the picture, and it adds force to the question whether belief in God,
where it exists outside the context of the special revelation, points
to a real knowledge of God or only to an *idea of God* which is a
product of the human mind. Does man really come to know God
by surveying the world in which he lives, or does he merely
project an idea of God to complement his understanding of his
own experienced finitude, much as a thirsty traveler in the desert
projects the idea of water?

(2) A knowledge of God by general revelation has often been
thought indispensable as a point of contact for the knowledge of
God which is given by special revelation. How could men receive

the saving knowledge of God in Christ at all, unless they had some previous knowledge of God? How could it have any meaning to them at all? This argument sounds extremely powerful, but it rests on the assumption that general revelation (if there be such a thing) and special revelation both carry us to the knowledge of the same God. This is just an assumption, and though it is taken for granted by many people, it may lie at the root of some of the well-known difficulties that accompany faith in God. It is not self-evident that the God who is believed in by Jews, or Moslems, or philosophical theists, is identical with the God and Father of our Lord Jesus Christ.

(3) The idea of general revelation seems to have the support of the Bible. Appeal is frequently made to such passages as Psalm 19:1 and Romans 1:19-20 (the latter cited in the Confession). It is a question, however, whether the psalmist and Paul are here referring to a knowledge of God in creation which they held to be available without revelation, or only to a knowledge which became available in the light of revelation. It should be noted that in the 19th Psalm the psalmist goes on to celebrate the light of the law of God (and this is virtually the Old Testament equivalent of "revelation") by which his eyes had been opened; and when Paul in Romans 1 speaks of the knowledge of God in creation, it is not as a knowledge which men actually have and from which they can advance to further knowledge, but as a knowledge they have lost; for by their failure to act on it they have forfeited it, and now, haunted by their lost knowledge of God, and unable to recover it, they are driven in their blindness to fashion idols (and ideas) as substitutes for the reality. (Rom. 1:21-25.) It should also be noted that in his speech at Athens, to which reference was made above, Paul appeals to the religiosity of the Athenians as evidence, not of a knowledge of God, but of ignorance of God, for which he calls them to repentance. (Acts 17:22-31.) The language in which the Confession refers to this subject clearly echoes that of Romans 1:19-20, where Paul is concerned to establish man's guilt, not his partial knowledge of God. But when it goes on to say that the manifestations of God in the created world

"are . . . not sufficient to give that knowledge of God, and of his will, which is necessary unto salvation," it seems to ascribe the failure to the inadequacy or partial nature of the general revelation—although the Scripture passages cited (I Cor. 1:21; 2:13-14) speak only of the failure of human wisdom. However that may be, it is clear that the Confession attaches little importance to the subject; for after this one brief reference to it, it immediately proceeds to special revelation, which it treats as its main theme.

How did God reveal himself? The Confession cites the phrase from Hebrews 1:1, "in divers manners," but it does not specify what those manners were. In the main, two things were involved. Revelation is customarily thought of as communication of truth in the form of words, whether it be by voices, visions, dreams, trances, oracles, ecstasies, or the like. This is suggested by the frequent Biblical references to "the word of God." But when we examine the Biblical record as a whole, it becomes clear that the revelation of God is not solely, and not primarily, verbal in form. God reveals himself primarily in his acts in history (his "mighty acts," Ps. 106:2, or his "wonderful works," Acts 2:11), and the words of revelation are the words which interpret those acts and convey their meaning to men. When the Bible speaks of the word of God, it does not refer only to speech or verbal communication. The word of God is the speaking side of his action.

The unity of act and word in revelation is clearly seen in the Old Testament. The great act of God to which, above all others, the faith of Israel was directed was the exodus from Egypt. The words of the "law" were the interpretation of this act; they spelled out the covenant relation which it established and which constituted the basis of Israel's obligation to God. The Ten Commandments do not state an abstract moral law; they define the terms of the covenant between Israel and the God of the exodus: "I am the Lord thy God, which have brought thee out of the land of Egypt, out of the house of bondage. Thou shalt . . ." (Exod. 20:2-17.) The relation of act and word can also be seen in the fact that the main body of the Old Testament consists of

books of history side by side with books of prophecy. The Jews
called both kinds of books prophetical, because, as they rightly
saw, the books we call historical are not historical in the ordinary
sense. The subject of these books is not the acts of Israel, but the
acts of God with Israel. Through these acts God was making
himself known to Israel; and it was the mission of the prophets
to interpret the acts and convey their meaning to the people. The
history was the text of the prophecy and the prophecy was the
commentary on the history.

"at sundry times." This phrase, also cited from Hebrews 1:1,
points to the fact that revelation was extended over a period
of time. But the Confession does not indicate—or only very
obliquely in the final clause of this paragraph—that the process
of God's revelation in history reached its climax and completion
in Jesus Christ. This is the main point of the passage in Hebrews,
which asserts that the same God who spoke at sundry times and
in divers manners to the fathers by the prophets has spoken to us
finally by his Son. It is the central message of the New Testament
that all the acts and words of God in his dealings with Israel
point forward to Jesus Christ, who is God's final and decisive act
and word in his own person. This is the heart of evangelical
Christian faith, and it ought to have been stated explicitly in the
Confession, because it is of critical importance, not only for faith
itself, but for the right understanding of revelation; for unless
revelation is seen in the light of its fulfillment in Christ, it will
tend to be construed as legal code (as in the Jewish synagogue)
rather than as the glad message of life and liberty, which it is.
(See II Cor. 3.)

"to declare that his will unto his church." The knowledge of
God which is given in revelation is of a practical, not a theoretical nature, and it is given within a relationship, which, in fact, it
constitutes. It is not given to all and sundry, but "unto his
church"—the name here referring not only to the Christian
church but also to the people of God in the Old Testament. God
chose this people to deal with; by his dealings with them he set
them in a special relation to himself, and he made himself known

to them within it. Knowledge of God is not like knowledge of geography or mathematics, which are open to everybody; it is given only to those whom he sets in a personal relation to himself. This is elaborated in Chapter VII of the Confession, which deals with God's covenant with man.

"and afterwards . . . to commit the same wholly unto writing; which maketh the Holy Scripture to be most necessary; those former ways of God's revealing his will unto his people being now ceased." After having described the revelation of the saving knowledge of God, the Confession now turns to the Bible, and it devotes the remainder of the chapter to it. The Confession makes it clear that the Bible is not simply identical with the revelation of God; there is a distinction between them; the revelation was given first, the Bible came *afterwards*—indeed, it was because of "those former ways of God's revealing his will . . . being now ceased" that the revelation was committed to writing. The Confession does not mean that the Bible is merely a record, in which the memory of revelation is preserved, and that those who read it are informed of an event in which they cannot themselves participate. Although "the former ways" of revelation have ceased, revelation is continued in another way. It is committed to the written record in such a way that the written record can convey it to those who use it, and bind them into the same relation to God ("the more sure establishment and comfort of the church") as those enjoyed who were contemporary with the original revelation. For us and for all who are not contemporary with the original revelation, the Bible is "most necessary" as our only means of access to it; and for this reason it can be called "the word of God written," as in Paragraph 2.

How does the Bible come to be recognized as the word of God and to occupy this unique position in the church? This is the question which the Confession answers in the following three paragraphs. It employs three important concepts, which must be carefully studied: canonicity, inspiration, and authority.

CF I,2   Under the name of Holy Scripture, or the word of

God written, are now contained all the books of the Old and New Testaments, which are these:

Of the Old Testament

Genesis
Exodus
Leviticus
Numbers
Deuteronomy
Joshua
Judges
Ruth
Samuel, I
Samuel, II
Kings, I
Kings, II
Chronicles, I
Chronicles, II
Ezra
Nehemiah
Esther
Job
Psalms
Proverbs
Ecclesiastes
The Song of Songs
Isaiah
Jeremiah
Lamentations
Ezekiel
Daniel
Hosea
Joel
Amos
Obadiah
Jonah
Micah
Nahum
Habakkuk
Zephaniah
Haggai
Zechariah
Malachi

Of the New Testament

The Gospel according to
  Matthew
  Mark
  Luke
  John
The Acts of the Apostles
The Epistles of Paul to
  the Romans
  Corinthians, I
  Corinthians, II
  Galatians
  Ephesians
  Philippians
  Colossians
Thessalonians, I
Thessalonians, II
To Timothy, I
To Timothy, II
To Titus
To Philemon
The Epistle to the Hebrews
The Epistle of James
The first and second
  Epistles of Peter
The first, second, and third
  Epistles of John
The Epistle of Jude
The Revelation

All which are given by inspiration of God, to be the rule of faith and life.

CF I,3 The books commonly called Apocrypha, not being of divine inspiration, are no part of the canon of the Scripture; and therefore are of no authority in the Church of God, nor to be any otherwise approved, or made use of, than other human writings.

CF I,4   The authority of the Holy Scripture, for which it ought to be believed and obeyed, dependeth not upon the testimony of any man or church, but wholly upon God (who is truth itself), the author thereof; and therefore it is to be received, because it is the word of God.

The books of the Old and New Testaments listed in Paragraph 2 compose the *canon* of Holy Scripture (although the term itself is not introduced till Par. 3). The word "canon" comes from the Greek, where it had a variety of meanings: originally a rod (perhaps a reed), it came to mean a ruler, then the line drawn by a ruler, finally the area marked off or enclosed by such a line. It was used in the church for the line which separates the books included in the Old and New Testaments from other books which were excluded; the books included were called canonical, in contrast to those which were excluded and which are called Apocrypha. When and on what grounds were these distinctions drawn, and what do they signify?

The history of the formation of the canon of Holy Scripture is too long and complicated to be related here, but the main facts may be briefly summarized. There were really two canons with distinct histories, the canon of the Old Testament and the canon of the New. In each case the problem arose because there were a considerable number of books in use besides those finally received into the canon, and responsible leaders in synagogue and church varied considerably in their attitudes toward them. As regards the Old Testament, the main problem was that the Septuagint, the Greek translation which was widely used by the Jews who were scattered throughout the Mediterranean world, contained a number of books which were not in the Hebrew Bible. Some of the rabbis also had serious doubts about the inclusion of some of the Hebrew books, such as Esther, Ecclesiastes, and the Song of Songs. These matters were settled at a rabbinical synod at Jamnia toward the end of the first century A.D., and the canon of the Old Testament was defined as we have it today.

The definition of the canon of the New Testament was also the outcome of protracted debates. There was a considerable body of Christian literature in circulation in the early church, and it was not easy to determine which books were to be selected for inclusion in the canon. Some of the most obstinate problems, which concerned books that were finally admitted (e.g., II Peter), do not appear to have been resolved before the second half of the fourth century.

The reception of the Old Testament canon in the Christian church forms yet another chapter in the story. So far as the included books are concerned, the rabbinical judgment appears to have been tacitly accepted, and no one appears to have questioned the propriety of this action or its consistency with the actual use which the New Testament makes of the Old, except Marcion, a famous heretic of the second century, whose extreme proposal to exclude the whole of the Old Testament from the Christian canon had probably a good deal to do with the church's determination to include the whole of it. A special question arose concerning the admission of the Apocrypha (the additional books contained in the Greek version of the Old Testament, which was used by the Jews of the Dispersion and by many members of the early church, who came from among them), and the church has still not agreed on a single answer to it. The Greek Orthodox Church has received them on the same footing as the canonical books; the Protestant Churches generally have rejected them; others, such as the Anglican Churches, have admitted them, but allow them only an inferior status.

The Confession bases the separation of the canonical from the apocryphal books on the ground that the former are "given by inspiration of God" while the latter are not "of divine inspiration." What is *inspiration?* Inspiration means that the Spirit of God was at work in the production of these writings. If, however, we ask, Precisely how did the Spirit of God inspire them? the Confession does not answer this question. Various *theories* have been devised regarding the inspiration of the Bible, but none of them can claim the endorsement of the Confession. The church's faith in the inspiration of the Bible cannot be tied up with any specific theory of inspiration. Theories of inspiration are attempts to explain it in terms of some supposedly analogous human activity or natural process. But if the inspiration is the work of the Spirit of God, it is unique and cannot be explained in terms of anything else.

The _authority_ of Scripture is dealt with in Paragraph 4. The Confession rejects any attempt to establish the authority of Scripture on extrinsic grounds. Here it is primarily opposing the argument used by some Roman Catholics in the controversies of the Reformation, that since the canon of Scripture was defined by the church, the authority of Scripture was conferred on it by the church. Scripture cannot have authority over the church as "the rule of faith and life" if it receives its authority from the church. The authority of Scripture derives solely from God who is "the author thereof"; that is, the source of its authority (not the literary author: the Confession does not imply that God wrote the Bible). The Bible is to be received as the word of God for no other reason than "because it is the word of God." The meaning of this apparently tautological statement is elucidated in the next paragraph.

CF I,5   We may be moved and induced by the testimony of the church to an high and reverent esteem for the Holy Scripture; and the heavenliness of the matter, the efficacy of the doctrine, the majesty of the style, the consent of all the parts, the scope of the whole (which is to give all glory to God), the full discovery it makes of the only way of man's salvation, the many other incomparable excellencies, and the entire perfection thereof, are arguments whereby it doth abundantly evidence itself to be the word of God; yet, notwithstanding, our full persuasion and assurance of the infallible truth and divine authority thereof, is from the inward work of the Holy Spirit, bearing witness by and with the word in our hearts.

34

"bearing witness by and with the word." The witness of the Spirit is distinct from the word, but at the same time it is elicited by the word and it attests the word. The Confession does not recognize any distinct new revelation by the Spirit (see Par. 6); the Spirit is witness to the revelation given once for all.

1,6   The whole counsel of God, concerning all things necessary for his own glory, man's salvation, faith, and life, is either expressly set down in Scripture, or by good and necessary consequence may be deduced from Scripture: unto which nothing at any time is to be added, whether by new revelations of the Spirit, or traditions of men. Nevertheless we acknowledge the inward illumination of the Spirit of God to be necessary for the saving understanding of such things as are revealed in the word; and that there are some circumstances concerning the worship of God, and government of the church, common to human actions and societies, which are to be ordered by the light of nature and Christian prudence, according to the general rules of the word, which are always to be observed.

...aving dealt with the canonicity, inspiration, and authority ...ripture, the Confession now turns to the practical bearing ...hese things on our use of Scripture. While the principal ...irement for the right and profitable use of the Bible is the ... witness of the Holy Spirit, the point of the remaining ...raphs of this chapter may be said to be that this does not ... us of the necessity of applying intelligence to the reading ... Bible. The idea that inspiration supersedes intelligence ... long history; it made its first appearance in the Christian ... at Corinth, where Paul vigorously opposed it (I Cor. ...), and it has frequently been revived. It underlies the ...le of those who have thought that the spiritual efficacy of ...ble is lost unless we read it, so to speak, with our eyes closed ...ir intelligence suppressed; but such a method receives no ...agement from the Confession, which proceeds to lay down

Though the authority of Scripture cannot be founded on "the testimony of any man or church" (Par. 4), the Confession recognizes that such testimony may serve a useful purpose in directing us toward the authority of Scripture. In other words, we cannot and do not accept the Bible as the word of God simply because other people say so; for that would be to set human authority above divine authority. Nevertheless, it is because other people say so that most people begin to listen to the Bible at all:

> Jesus loves me! this I know,
> For my mother told me so.

This is how it begins for most of us. But it must not and cannot end there. However deeply we may be indebted to it, no mere human testimony is sufficient, whether it be the formal testimony of the church in its preaching and teaching, or the informal testimony of a parent or friend. And, of course, no human being (except the Pope) would expect us to accept the truth on the strength of his "I say so" alone; they would all direct us to the Bible.

Can we then by reading the Bible itself discover anything in it that proves it is the word of God? The answer which the Confession gives to this question must be carefully observed. It recites an eloquent list of the qualities and characteristics of the Bible, but it is careful to point out that, though these are highly suggestive, they cannot be held to prove that it is the word of God; they are presumptive evidence, but they are not conclusive proof. This is the more remarkable, because the language used in describing the qualities of Scripture clearly reflects an uncritical attitude to it; yet, even though these qualities are thought to add up to "entire perfection," they still do not furnish a sufficient ground for the authority of the Bible as the word of God. The reason is that all these qualities of Scripture which might impress a reader—and he would be an obtuse reader if some of them did not impress him—are matters of human judgment; and the divine authority of Scripture depends on human judgment just as little as, or even less than, it does on human testimony. The

Confession allows that human judgment, like human testimony, can take us part of the way; it can give us a strong impression of the Bible. But this is not proof of its divine authority. It is a well-known fact that people can be impressed with the Bible without accepting its authority as the word of God. Indeed, there is general agreement among persons of literary sensibility that the Bible is a profoundly impressive book, and some of them would be willing to say that it is inspired—in the same way that other great works of literature are inspired. The Confession is emphatic that the authority of the Bible does not rest on any impression or judgment we may form concerning its contents or style. The proof of its divine authority "is from the inward work of the Holy Spirit, bearing witness by and with the word in our hearts."

The doctrine of "the inner witness of the Holy Spirit," as it is called,[1] completes and rounds off the doctrine of inspiration. It makes it conclusively clear why the Confession, as was indicated above, does not elaborate a theory of inspiration. The inspiration of the Bible is not a matter of theory; it is a matter of faith. And faith cannot be made to rest on theory; it is always faith in God—and here, specifically, faith in God in the person of the Holy Spirit. The doctrine of the inner witness of the Holy Spirit means that we cannot truly grasp the inspiration of the Bible until we are ourselves inspired by the same Spirit by whom the writers of the Bible were inspired; we cannot truly recognize the authority of the Bible as the word of God until God himself speaks his word to us through the Bible.

The inspiration of the Bible cannot be separated from the message of the Bible. The message of the Bible was defined in Paragraph 1 as "that knowledge of God, and of his will, which is necessary unto salvation," and it was shown that this is not like a knowledge of theoretical truth, which can be received in an attitude of detachment, but is a knowledge which involves those

who receive it in a personal and communal relati
It was given through God's revealing acts, and it
to writing so that it could be continued beyond th
original revealing acts. But a knowledge that esta
relation with God cannot be conveyed merely by
or oral report. The Bible mediates it to us, but t
effect it. This is the work of God himself in th
Holy Spirit, who uses the written word of t
medium through which he speaks to us the liv
brings us into living relation with himself. Th
inner witness of the Holy Spirit means that wh
word is to accomplish its purpose with us, i
inspiration, but prayer. The meaning is ad
(though the doctrine itself is not named) b
Shorter Catechism, in answer to the question
to be read and heard, that it may become effe
—"That the word may become effectual to
attend thereunto with diligence, preparation
it with faith and love, lay it up in our hear
our lives." (SC 90.)[2]

---

[1] The name comes from Calvin, to whom the church is chiefly indebted for the formulation of this doctrine (*Institutes*, Book I, Chapter VII).

[2] The impulse to form theories of inspiration
encouragement from the manner in which the Cor
as the hallmark of canonical Scripture in Paragrap
books are inspired, and the apocryphal not, this
between them. Indeed, this was more in the na
other differences of a more palpable order. Whe
which books were to be received into the canon
which to be excluded, it did not confine itself
inspired? The principal test it used was that of
test for the Old Testament had been that of
in a somewhat broad sense). The distinctive fea
is that their authors were actual participants
were themselves *in* the truth of which they wr
that they were commissioned to be witnesses
inspiration of their writings ought not to be i
to the truth; in other words, it should not b
happened to them only when they wrote, bu
in their being apostles.

certain guiding principles for the intelligent use of the Bible.

An intelligent use of Scripture depends upon the observance of certain critical distinctions in regard to its contents. The first of these, which is the theme of this paragraph, is <u>the distinction between what the Bible says and what it does not say</u>. What the Bible says is summarized here as "the whole counsel of God, concerning all things necessary for his own glory, man's salvation, faith, and life." Do these things include everything in the Bible? The answer of the Confession is given indirectly, but it is quite clear; these are the things which form the themes of the following chapters. <u>These are the things for which we go to the Bible. But the Confession does not suggest that the Bible is an oracle, or encyclopedia, to which we can go for answers to questions on all sorts of subjects.</u> On the contrary, it states that even the answers to questions about things necessary for salvation are in some cases obtainable only by logical deduction from the express utterances of Scripture (the doctrine of the Trinity would be an example; see CF II, 3); and there are some questions on which some authoritative guidance might well have been considered desirable—questions concerning how we should worship, and whether the church should be governed by bishops or presbyters —and to which the Bible gives no answers, and we are left to depend on sanctified common sense. Nevertheless, the Confession is careful to distinguish between the occasional necessity of employing logical inference to obtain the divine message of salvation from the Bible and the view that that message is so incompletely delivered in the Bible that it requires supplementing, either by additional revelations, or by extra-canonical traditions. The former is the position of the "Spiritualist" sects, the latter is that of the Roman Catholic Church. Against both, the Confession asserts the sufficiency and finality of the Biblical revelation; it is fundamental to evangelical faith that God in Christ has done "all things necessary for . . . man's salvation."

CF I,7   All things in Scripture are not alike plain in themselves, nor alike clear unto all; yet those things which are necessary to be known, believed, and observed, for salvation, are so clearly propounded and opened in some place of Scripture or other, that not only the learned, but the unlearned, in a due use of the ordinary means, may attain unto a sufficient understanding of them.

The Confession here points to another critical distinction which an intelligent reading of Scripture must recognize: some **parts of Scripture are clear, others are obscure.** The recommendation of the Confession on this point is eminently commonsensible. It affirms that the deliverances of the Bible on its main theme (here described as "those things which are necessary to be known, believed, and observed, for salvation") are clear enough to be understood by any person of normal intelligence; the inference is that the obscurities are found in matters of secondary or peripheral importance, and that they may be left to those who are minded to concern themselves with them.

CF I,8   The Old Testament in Hebrew (which was the native language of the people of God of old), and the New Testament in Greek (which at the time of the writing of it was most generally known to the nations), being immediately inspired by God, and by his singular care and providence kept pure in all ages, are therefore authentical; so as in all controversies of religion the church is finally to appeal unto them. But because these original tongues are not known to all the people of God who have right unto, and interest in, the Scriptures, and are commanded, in the fear of God, to read and search them, therefore they are to be translated into the language of every people unto which they come, that the word of God dwelling plentifully in all, they may worship him in an acceptable manner, and, through patience and comfort of the Scriptures, may have hope.

The statement that the original texts of the Biblical writings (like those of any writings) are superior in authority to all later copies and translations is sound in principle, but difficult problems arise when we attempt to apply it. For though it may well be true that the text of the Bible has on the whole been preserved, under God's providence, with a remarkable degree of purity, there is no Biblical manuscript in existence which can be held to furnish the authentic text; the original autographs, which presumably contained it, are lost, and appeal to them would be a counsel of despair. The most that can be said is that the text which can be reconstructed from the oldest surviving manuscripts is nearer authentic than any other. Apart from questions of text, it should also be said that the original languages of the Bible provide more authentic expressions of the thought of the Biblical writers than any others. But the Confession reaffirms the great conviction of the Reformation that the Bible can be translated into the native language of every people without serious loss or danger. In contrast to the Roman Catholic Church at that time, the Reformers held that it was both safe and salutary to make the Bible accessible to all and let it convey its message to all in their own languages. Today the Roman Catholic Church also encourages its members to read the Bible in the vernacular, provided they read it in versions authorized or edited by the Church. It is scarcely necessary to add that, if translation of the Bible is necessary and desirable, so also is re-translation, as and when better manuscript sources of the original text come to light and the language of existing translations becomes archaic and unintelligible.

CF I,9   The infallible rule of interpretation of Scripture, is the Scripture itself; and therefore, when there is a question about the true and full sense of any scripture (which is not manifold, but one), it may be searched and known by other places that speak more clearly.

The basic rule for the interpretation of Scripture, which the Confession states here, has often been expressed in the phrase: Scripture is its own interpreter. It has two meanings, one negative, the other positive. Negatively, it prohibits the application to Scripture of principles of interpretation (or hermeneutics) which may be applicable to books dealing with other subjects. The principles of interpretation applied to any book must be appropriate to the subject of the book, and the subject of Scripture is unique. Positively, the rule states that the meaning of any particular passage of Scripture must be sought in the light of the general meaning of Scripture as a whole, which, as was stated in Paragraph 7, is sufficiently clear. This principle was sometimes called "the analogy of faith" (a literal rendering of the final phrase in Romans 12:6).

"which is not manifold, but one." This is a reference to the allegorical method of interpreting Scripture, which was much used in the pre-Reformation church. The theory was that Scripture has a variety of meanings—the meaning which lies on the surface, so to speak, and two or three other meanings, which lie at different levels below the surface—and the allegorical method was employed to bring these out. The Confession rejects this conception, and rightly so, since it makes it impossible to determine with certainty what the true meaning of Scripture is. It was said of the allegorical method that it makes Scripture into a "wax nose" which the interpreter can twist into any shape he likes.

CF I,10   The Supreme Judge, by which all controversies of religion are to be determined, and all decrees of councils, opinions of ancient writers, doctrines of men, and private spirits, are to be examined, and in whose sentence we are to rest, can be no other but the Holy Spirit speaking in the Scripture.

The Confession concludes this long chapter with a fuller statement on the authority of Scripture, which it has previously affirmed in a general way in Paragraph 2. Here it asserts that the authority of Scripture is superior to that of certain other claimants to authority which may be, and in some cases have been, recognized in the church. "Decrees of councils" and "opinions of ancient writers" (i.e., the church Fathers) refer to the creedal and dogmatic tradition of the early church, which is regarded by Roman Catholics and Anglicans as possessing a degree of authority equal, or even superior, to that of Scripture. "Doctrines of men" probably refers to doctrinal innovations that made their appearance at later dates in the Roman Catholic Church. "Private spirits" refers to the claims to have received additional revelations from the Spirit of God which were advanced by the "Spirituals" or "Enthusiasts" of the Reformation period. The Confession does not mean that these are destitute of authority altogether and are to be taken no account of at all in the church. It means that whatever degree of authority they possess, it is subordinate to the authority of Scripture and may not be elevated above it. The relation between them may be compared to that between the first commandment and the fifth: just as the supreme authority of God does not negate the relative authority of parents, so the supreme authority of Scripture allows a relative weight to the authority of tradition, etc. The reference to "decrees of councils" should be specially noted, because the Confession of Faith itself may be considered to fall into this category. (See CF XXXIII, 3.) Finally, the Confession repeats that the supreme authority, to which all others are subject, is "the Holy Spirit speaking in the Scripture." This does not mean that the letter of Scripture is of no consequence; but it is a warning against the literalistic attitude toward the Bible which supposes that controversial issues can be settled by the citation of proof texts. The Confession points a more excellent way.

▪ chapter II

OF GOD, AND OF THE HOLY TRINITY

This is one of the most difficult chapters in the Confession, as its subject is the most exalted, and some preliminary observations seem called for. The reader is likely to be overwhelmed by the mass of complex detail which is presented in these paragraphs and to find that in the end he has received no clear impression of what they are intended to convey to him. In cases like this it is often helpful to ask ourselves, What is the question that is being answered? In this case that is not hard to find, since we have it in both the Catechisms. Both the Catechisms reproduce the substance of the first two paragraphs of this chapter, in greatly abbreviated form, in answer to the question, What is God? (LC 7; SC 4.)

What is God? Is this the right question to begin with? It may sound innocent enough, but we must consider what it implies. When we ask the question, What is God? we imply that it is possible for us to observe God and describe him much as we might describe someone we had seen in the street. Any such description would take the form of a mental image or picture or idea of God. But this is what, in the second commandment, we are forbidden to make, for the prohibition of images applies not only to material images, but also, as the Larger Catechism points out, to "the making any representation of God . . . inwardly in our mind." (LC 109.) And the reason for the prohibition is simply that God cannot be imagined (i.e., represented in an image), because he is not "there" to be observed, like any created object. God is hidden from us. We know him only as he reveals himself to us (see CF I, 1); and when God reveals himself to us, it is in his own image, not one of our devising. We cannot form an image of God, because we are creatures and all our imaginations are creaturely. God has made himself known to us by confronting us in his own authentic image. (Heb. 1:3.)

This is the real meaning of the doctrine of the Trinity, which is stated in Paragraph 3, and which ought therefore to be considered first.

CF II,3   In the unity of the Godhead there be three persons of one substance, power, and eternity: God the Father, God the Son, and God the Holy Ghost. The Father is of none, neither begotten nor proceeding; the Son is eternally begotten of the Father; the Holy Ghost eternally proceeding from the Father and the Son.

The meaning of the doctrine of the Trinity can best be understood if it is taken as the answer to the question, Who is God? This is really the question of primary importance; for as the Bible makes abundantly plain, the greatest temptation of men in all ages is the confusion of God with not-God. This is the danger we are warned against in the first commandment, and if we are to avoid it, it is clearly imperative that we know who God is, and how he is distinguished from not-God. The doctrine of the Trinity is the formula in which the Christian church, after long and careful consideration, decided that the answer which is given to this all-important question in the Biblical revelation had to be stated, in order to protect it from misunderstanding and confusion. Who is God? God is he who has revealed himself in Christ through the Holy Spirit. This is the basic affirmation of Christian faith; and it is the necessary implications of this basic affirmation which were formulated in the doctrine of the Trinity.

The ecclesiastical formulation of the doctrine of the Trinity was accomplished in two stages, and a brief review of them may help to bring out its meaning. Christian faith, as its name indicates, is faith in Christ; but Christian faith in Christ is faith that "God was in Christ," as Paul sums it up. (II Cor. 5:19.) In Christ we have to do with God himself, not merely with a man sent from God, like John the Baptist, or one of the prophets. (Compare Mark 8:27-29.) It would have been easier to think of him in that way, as a prophet, or even as some kind of angel, but the church rejected all such suggestions, because it saw that though they might simplify the problem for thought, they would be inconsistent with the faith that in Christ we have God himself present with us and doing for us what only God can do. Under stress of controversy the church was forced more and more to the conclusion that this faith must have its ground in the being of God himself, in some unparalleled complexity or repetition whereby his being God is not limited to his being God in himself but also includes his being God with us, without detriment to his being one God. The problem was to find a formula that would express this plurality-in-unity. The Biblical terms, Father and Son, were not adequate; they could be used to designate God and Christ in their distinctness—and even in that use, it was realized, they could not be taken literally—but they could not express the unity between God and Christ (some people were willing to call Christ the Son of God, but insisted that he was of an inferior order of being). The Council of Nicaea, which was called to deal with the issue in A.D. 325, adopted a highly technical Greek term, *homo-ousios,* and this is translated in the phrase "of one substance" in our Confession. (Elsewhere it is rendered "consubstantial" or "co-essential.") But the translation is misleading in so far as it suggests that "Godhead" or divinity is a kind of substance of which God and Christ are composed, in the same way as carbon is the substance of which both diamond and graphite are composed. The Greek word means literally "the same in being," and when the Council put this word in the Nicene Creed it intended to say that the distinction between the Father and the Son is not a distinction between two beings but a distinction between two ways of God's being God.

The Council of Nicaea was concerned only with defining the relation between the Father and the Son, and it gave no consideration to the question of the Holy Spirit. But once the implications of the church's faith in Christ had been clarified, it was soon realized that the same implications were present in the church's faith in the Holy Spirit. The church recognized in the coming of the Spirit the continued presence of Christ the Lord. Indeed, the presence of Christ could be recognized in no other way. (I Cor. 12:3.) To have the Spirit was to have Christ, and to have Christ was to have God. It became clear, therefore, that it would be necessary to repeat what the Council of Nicaea had found it necessary to say in order to protect the church's faith in Christ, with reference to the Holy Spirit; and this was done by the Council of Constantinople in A.D. 381, which declared in effect (though carefully avoiding the term, which had become distasteful to many in the church) that the Spirit is also "of one substance" with the Father and the Son.

The second stage in the development of the doctrine of the Trinity consisted in the quest for a term to express the distinction which has to be recognized between the Father, the Son, and the Holy Spirit, within the unity. For, while we have God present with us in Christ through the Holy Spirit, and this, not as three distinct presences, but as one presence, there is also a distinction, which may be expressed in this way: in Christ we have God *with* us, and in the Holy Spirit we have God *in* us, without his ever ceasing to be God *over* us. This threefoldness in the modes of his presence must have its ground in some kind of distinction in the being of God himself. But once more, the problem was to find a term for it. The problem was solved in a somewhat artificial manner by taking another technical Greek word and setting it apart for this special purpose. This is the word translated "person" in English, but the translation is inaccurate and misleading; "person" in modern English means a distinct, self-conscious individual, but clearly it cannot bear this meaning in the formula, "three persons in the Godhead," because that would make the Trinity into tritheism (three gods). It has been recognized almost from the beginning that "person" is a makeshift in this context, but no one has succeeded in finding a better word to take its place, and it seems probable that "person" will continue to be

"Person"

used. Only, it should be remembered that the word is an attempt to express something which it is beyond the resources of human language to express, namely, a distinction within the unity of the being of God to which we have no parallel in our experience as his creatures.

Is this doctrine of the Trinity necessary? Unitarians say No. But since their rejection of the doctrine rests on rejection of the premise on which it was based ("God was in Christ"), their position need not be considered here. There are some, however, who accept the basic position of Christian faith, that God was in Christ, but who deny that this points to any distinctions in the being of God. Those who take this view argue that the distinctions pertain only to God in his relation to the world. They say that in his relation to the world God has revealed himself as Father, Son, and Holy Spirit, but these distinctions are tied up with the nature and purpose of his dealings with the world— they are purely "economic" ("economy" was used in the ancient church as a comprehensive term for God's dealings with the world), not essential, or ontological, i.e., they do not enter into the inner being of God. This view, which is superficially attractive, was rejected by the church, partly because the evidence of the New Testament points to an essential rather than an economic Trinity, partly because a purely economic view of the Trinity would introduce a contradiction between God as he is in himself and God as he has revealed himself to us, and would thus destroy our confidence in the authenticity of revelation. The church was constrained to think that the relations between the Father, the Son, and the Holy Spirit, which are manifested in the economic order, are the counterpart of relations which belong to the eternal being of God, or, in other words, that the three modes in which he is present to us correspond to three modes in which he is present to himself.

It is another question how far we may go in the definition of these "inner-trinitarian relations." In the final sentence of this paragraph the Confession reproduces the language of one attempted definition which was propounded in the ancient church and has enjoyed a wide currency. This was an attempt to make the threeness intelligible in terms of derivation from an original unity, without involving the thought of sequence. The Father was thought of as the primal source or "fountain of Godhead," and the Son and the Spirit as originating from the Father, who is himself without origin ("unoriginate"). The modes and sources of the origination of the Son and the Spirit were then distinguished in this way: the Son is *begotten* of the Father, while the Spirit *proceeds* from the Father and the Son; and both the begetting (or "generation") and the procession were said to be eternal, i.e., they do not involve succession, like the generation of a human son from a human father, but are more like the generation of light from a flame, or water from a spring (these were the favorite illustrations). No definitive answer could be found to the question how generation differs from procession, but that was not important. The terms were taken from the New Testament (John 1:14, 18; 15:26), and the main purpose for which they were used was to establish the fundamental difference between the relation of both the Son and the Spirit to the Father and that of all other beings; all other beings are created, they are not begotten of, or proceeding from God; the Son and the Spirit are one in being with him.

It may be added that the primary concern behind the doctrine of the Trinity is the unity of God. The doctrine, which ought really to be called the Tri-unity (like the German *Dreieinigkeit*), stated that God is three-in-one, rather than one-in-three; the emphasis is on the one-ness, not the three-ness. Its purpose is to guard the basic Christian faith that in Christ and in the Holy Spirit we have God himself, and though we have to distinguish between God in himself, God with us, and God in us, it is always the one God himself with whom we have to do. By the same token, the doctrine guards the unity of the works of God. It is not intended to point to a division of labor within the Godhead, as if God the Father alone were responsible for the work of creation, the Son for salvation, and the Holy Spirit for sanctification, but rather to stress the fact that, although each of these works is sometimes associated in a special manner with one of the three "persons," each is the work of the triune God, who is wholly present in all his works, and through all of them is pursuing his one eternal purpose.

CF II,1   There is but one only living and true God, who is infinite in being and perfection, a most pure spirit, invisible, without body, parts, or passions, immutable, immense, eternal, incomprehensible, almighty; most wise, most holy, most free, most absolute, working all things according to the counsel of his own immutable and most righteous will, for his own glory; most loving, gracious, merciful, long-suffering, abundant in goodness and truth, forgiving iniquity, transgression, and sin; the rewarder of them that diligently seek him; and withal most just and terrible in his judgments; hating all sin, and who will by no means clear the guilty.

CF II,2   God hath all life, glory, goodness, blessedness, in and of himself; and is alone in and unto himself all-sufficient, not standing in need of any creatures which he hath made, nor deriving any glory from them, but only manifesting his own glory in, by, unto, and upon them: he is the alone fountain of all being, of whom, through whom, and to whom, are all things; and hath most sovereign dominion over them, to do by them, for them, or upon them, whatsoever himself pleaseth. In his sight all things are open and manifest; his knowledge is infinite, infallible, and independent upon the creature; so as nothing is to him contingent or uncertain. He is most holy in all his counsels, in all his works, and in all his commands. To him is due from angels and men, and every other creature, whatsoever worship, service, or obedience he is pleased to require of them.

The answer of Christian faith to the question, Who is God?,

which is given in the doctrine of the Trinity (Par. 3), has prepared us better to understand what is said in these two paragraphs in answer to the question, What is God? It will be observed that the qualities or attributes ascribed to God in the first paragraph fall into two groups: those listed first, as far as the word "glory," pertain to the being of God in himself (they have been called the absolute attributes); those which follow pertain to God in his relation to the world (they have been called the relative attributes). This is the paradox which lies at the very heart of the Christian faith, and which is enshrined in the doctrine of the Trinity, namely, that God, who is infinite, almighty, sovereign, and sufficient to himself, condescends to enter into relation with us, his creatures, and in his dealings with us shows himself most loving, gracious, and merciful. It is unfortunate that the Confession fails to bring this out as clearly as it might have done, and the failure assumes a more serious aspect in Paragraph 2, where it allows the relative attributes to be swallowed up in the absolute; for this paragraph seems to say that in his dealings with his creatures God acts according to those attributes which pertain to his being God in himself—independence, omniscience, omnipotence, etc.; but of the attributes of love, grace, mercy, longsuffering, etc., which are ascribed to him in Paragraph 1, not a trace is to be found. This failure, which reappears at other places in the Confession (notably in the following chapter), is the consequence of a failure to grasp the central truth, which the doctrine of the Trinity was framed to protect, that the God of Christian faith is "the God and Father of our Lord Jesus Christ." (Eph. 1:3; I Peter 1:3; II Cor. 1:3, etc.) The Confession undoubtedly intends and professes to describe the God who is revealed in Christ, but, failing to discern the actual pattern of his being, it ends in describing another God, who is unrevealed, and who lacks the attributes of the God and Father of our Lord Jesus Christ. Thus it actually imperils the faith it asserts, that "there is but one only living and true God," because it fails to concentrate attention on the authentic image of himself which God has given us in Jesus Christ.

The danger of fabricating images of God has been referred to in the previous paragraph. These two paragraphs may furnish a clue to the root from which the impulse arises. Most of the absolute attributes ascribed to God are expressed in negative or superlative terms, and this clearly suggests comparison with other beings, such as ourselves, who lack them completely, or possess them in a lower degree; in other words, they are saying that God is wholly other than, or very much more of, what we are. But when we use this kind of language, are we saying something about God, or only about ourselves? Are we setting up an image of God, which is only a projection of ourselves or a compensation for the deficiencies of our own being? The danger is that when men say that there is one God and that he is possessed of all the qualities enumerated in the list, they may really be saying nothing more than that they themselves, who are not God, are many, finite, imperfect, impure, visible, corporeal, composite, passionate, changeable, local, temporal, transparent, weak, foolish, common, determined by alien forces, and subservient to alien wills. The only authentic knowledge of God is that which he has given us in his revelation of himself in Jesus Christ through the Holy Spirit. Here he has given us his own true image of himself, not as our contrary, or our complement, but as our Saviour, the One who is wholly other, just because he is wholly akin. This is the paradox that informs the Christian knowledge of God and his attributes. It is because he reveals himself to us and relates himself to us that we know him to be absolute and sufficient unto himself; for he imparts himself to us. It is because he is most loving that we know him to be most free; for he loves us freely. It is because he is most gracious and merciful that we know him to be most just and terrible in his judgments; for he judges by forgiving iniquity, transgression, and sin. It is because he does all things necessary for our salvation that we know him to have all glory in himself and to derive none from us; for he "hath called us unto his eternal glory by Christ Jesus." (I Peter 5:10.)

■ chapter III

OF GOD'S ETERNAL DECREES[1]

CF III,1   God from all eternity did by the most wise and holy counsel of his own will, freely and unchangeably ordain whatsoever comes to pass; yet so as thereby neither is God the author of sin; nor is violence offered to the will of the creatures, nor is the liberty or contingency of second causes taken away, but rather established.

CF III,2   Although God knows whatsoever may or can come to pass, upon all supposed conditions; yet hath he not decreed anything because he foresaw it as future, or as that which would come to pass, upon such conditions.

CF III,3   By the decree of God, for the manifestation of his glory, some men and angels are predestinated unto everlasting life, and others fore-ordained to everlasting death.

CF III,4   These angels and men, thus predestinated and fore-ordained, are particularly and unchangeably designed; and their number is so certain and definite that it cannot be either increased or diminished.

---

[1] The original text of the Confession had "Decree," and the singular has been retained in the text used in most Presbyterian Churches. The substitution of the plural was probably made in order to bring the Confession into line with the Catechisms, both of which ask, "What are the decrees of God?" (LC 12, SC 7.)

CF III,5   Those of mankind that are predestinated unto life, God, before the foundation of the world was laid, according to his eternal and immutable purpose, and the secret counsel and good pleasure of his will, hath chosen in Christ, unto everlasting glory, out of his free grace and love alone, without any foresight of faith or good works, or perseverance in either of them, or any other thing in the creature, as conditions, or causes moving him thereunto; and all to the praise of his glorious grace.

CF III,6   As God hath appointed the elect unto glory, so hath he, by the eternal and most free purpose of his will, fore-ordained all the means thereunto. Wherefore they who are elected being fallen in Adam, are redeemed by Christ, are effectually called unto faith in Christ by his Spirit working in due season; are justified, adopted, sanctified, and kept by his power through faith unto salvation. Neither are any other redeemed by Christ, effectually called, justified, adopted, sanctified, and saved, but the elect only.

CF III,7   The rest of mankind, God was pleased, according to the unsearchable counsel of his own will, whereby he extendeth or withholdeth mercy as he pleaseth, for the glory of his sovereign power over his creatures, to pass by, and to ordain them to dishonor and wrath for their sin, to the praise of his glorious justice.

CF III,8   The doctrine of this high mystery of predestination is to be handled with special prudence and care, that men attending the will of God revealed in his word, and yielding obedience thereunto, may, from the certainty of their effectual vocation, be assured of their eternal election. So shall this doctrine afford matter of praise, reverence, and admiration of God; and of humility, diligence, and abundant consolation to all that sincerely obey the gospel.

The awesome doctrine of the "double decree," or "double predestination," which has often been regarded as the distinctive feature of the Reformed faith, is no longer held by the Presbyterian Churches in the form in which it is set forth in this chapter. This is one of the points at which several of these Churches have adopted declaratory statements regarding the sense in which they accept the formulation of the doctrine of the Confession. The doctrine still has its defenders among devotees of traditional orthodoxy, but not even among them is it cherished with any degree of enthusiasm. And in the preaching and teaching of the Churches generally it would seem that the recommendation, given in Paragraph 8, that the subject be handled wth special caution, has been taken to mean that it should be passed over in complete silence.

It would be unwise, however, to neglect the doctrine without further inquiry into its significance. The prominent place which it held so long in the Reformed faith would itself seem to be an indication that some truth of vital importance to faith lies hidden at its core, and that it might be worth the effort to see if this kernel can be extracted and disengaged from the forbidding husk in which it is enclosed. But before this is done, it is necessary to show why the doctrine is no longer acceptable in the form in which it is presented in the Confession. Four reasons may be given:

(1) The first is rather general, but not without some weight. No reader who compares the statement of the doctrine in the Confession with the Biblical passages on which it is ostensibly founded can fail to notice a profound difference in tone between them. This is especially evident if we take the two passages, Ephesians 1:3-14 and Romans 8:29-30, which together furnish practically all the terms employed in the formulation of the doctrine (with one significant exception which will be noted later): both breathe an air of exultant joy; both exemplify what has been called "truth that sings." The chapter in the Confession, by contrast, breathes an air of dread and doom, and it ends with the

advice to handle the subject with extreme caution. There is no
suggestion of caution in Ephesians 1 and Romans 8; there, if ever,
the apostle is letting himself go.

(2) The idea that God has foreordained the reprobate to everlasting death, which is the chief stumbling-stone, leans heavily on
the passage in Romans 9: 19-23 which speaks of "vessels of wrath
fitted to destruction"; but the passage will not bear the interpretation that has been imposed on it, for apart from the fact that it
is not stated *by whom* the vessels were fitted to destruction (as was
noted by some members of the Westminster Assembly), the context makes it clear that the destruction, to which they were fitted,
cannot be equated with everlasting death, for the theme of this
entire section of the Epistle is the ultimate triumph of God's
saving purpose with Israel in spite of all temporary and apparent
setbacks. The use of the phrase in the Confession to support the
doctrine of reprobation is a signal example of the danger of taking a text out of its context. Even the immediate context of the
text should have been sufficient to prevent this; for it speaks not
of how God effected the destruction of those vessels, but of how
he "endured [them] with much long-suffering," or patience. And
this is the keynote of the whole three chapters (Rom. 9-11) in
which Paul treats of the destiny of Israel in the purpose of God:
it is not the fixity of his resolve in making an unalterable separation between the elect and the reprobate and adhering to it
through thick and thin; it is the infinite patience and resourcefulness of his grace, not only in pursuing his purpose with Israel,
but in extending it to include the Gentiles by the strategy of the
cross, in which the temporary rejection of the elect proves the
means to the ultimate salvation of the reprobate. Paul mounts up
to the triumphant conclusion that "all Israel shall be saved"
(Rom. 11:26), because he knew, in the light of the cross, that none
are saved but by the mercy of God, and they are saved, not because they are savable, but because they are damnable: "For
God hath concluded them all in unbelief, that he might have
mercy upon all" (Rom. 11:32). It may be added that this is also
the theme of the famous passage in Jeremiah (18:1-10) about the

potter and the pot, which has often been misunderstood (and of which we have an echo in Romans 9:20-24): the point is not the helplessness of the pot in the hand of the potter, it is the resourcefulness of the potter with the pot in his hand; for what the prophet observed when he watched the potter at work was that when he turned out a vessel "fitted to destruction" he did *not* destroy it, "he made it again another vessel" (Rom. 9:22; Jer. 18:4). And the lesson he drew from this was that in his dealings with the nations God does not operate mechanically according to a fixed formula, like a petty official who is bound by red tape; God is free to modify his action from day to day according to the reaction of those with whom he is dealing. God is indeed free "to make one vessel unto honour, and another unto dishonour"; but the truth which the prophet divined, and the apostle discerned more clearly in the light of the gospel of Christ, is that God uses his freedom so that even the vessel which is good for nothing is not excluded from his purpose of salvation.

(3) If the question be asked, How did the Biblical testimony to the resourcefulness of grace come to be transformed into the theological doctrine of double predestination? the answer would seem to be that those who framed the doctrine were misled by a false model. The clue is to be found in the term which they used to entitle the doctrine and which dominates their interpretation of it, namely, "decree." This term is absent from the New Testament passages which deal with election. "Decree" belongs to the language of the Old Testament, where it is used with reference to God six times; in four places it is used in connection with what are now commonly called laws of nature (Job 28:26; Ps. 148:6; Prov. 8:29; Jer. 5:22), in one place its meaning is uncertain (Zeph. 2:2), and in only one does it refer to election—in that case the election of the Messianic king (Ps. 2:7). The absence of the word from the New Testament is no accident; for it suggests a fixed and unalterable enactment, which is not appropriate to what the men of the New Testament had come to know of the freedom of the grace of God in Jesus Christ. The New Testament term is "purpose" (noun and verb are used seven times in the context of

election, Romans 8:28; 9:11; Ephesians 1:9, 11; 3:11; II Timothy 1:9), and it indicates that in this matter of election God is actively pursuing a goal which he has set before him rather than mechanically carrying out a decision which he took once long ago.

(4) The criticism which has just been made points to a major deficiency in the implied conception of eternity and its relation to time. The relation of time and eternity is an extremely difficult problem and one which is probably insoluble by the human mind (which belongs to the temporal order). Without going into all the ramifications of the problem, however, it is possible to say that there is fairly general agreement on one point, namely, that it is inadequate to think of eternity as endless extension of time. Eternity differs from time in quality as well as quantity; it is not just a great deal more of the same kind of thing, it is a different kind of thing altogether. Now the authors of the Confession show no awareness of this; they view the difference between time and eternity in terms of quantity only. But even if it be true that the Bible shares this "naive" view of eternity as endless extension of time,[2] the Confession employs it in a very one-sided way; for the Bible views eternity as (at least) the extension of time *in both directions;* it is both before and after time; God is "from everlasting to everlasting" (Ps. 90:2), he is the "Alpha and Omega" (Rev. 1:8), "the first, and . . . the last" (Isa. 44:6), and he besets us "behind and before" (Ps. 139:5). In the Confession, on the other hand, God is confined, so to speak, to that dimension of his eternity which is antecedent to time, and the relation of his will to the events which come to pass in time is conceived purely in terms of before and after: "God from all eternity did . . . ordain whatsoever comes to pass." (Par. 1.) The consequence is that the doctrine assumes the cast of a deterministic philosophy, in which there is no real place for human freedom, despite verbal protestations to the contrary. But the decisive objection to this form of the doctrine is not that it is destructive of human freedom; it is

---

[2] Compare Oscar Cullmann, *Christ and Time* (The Westminster Press, 1950).

that it denies the freedom of God—that is, his freedom to be God in all the dimensions of his eternity and to pursue his eternal purpose in time and through time. If all things that come to pass have been determined by God's decree from all eternity, then, once the decree has been fixed, God becomes, in effect, his own executor.[3] But such a God is not eternal in the full sense of the word; he is only pre-temporal.

The root of the doctrine is undoubtedly the sovereignty of the grace of God as it is exhibited in his saving work in Christ, and its basic intention is to trace this grace to its eternal ground in the will of God. This is confirmed by the history of the doctrine; for it was first formulated by Augustine, and it was developed out of his profound conviction that the salvation of men is wholly the work of God and they themselves contribute nothing to it. As one of his favorite texts puts it, "it is not of him that willeth, nor of him that runneth, but of God that sheweth mercy." (Rom. 9:16; the Revised Standard Version has, "it depends not upon man's will or exertion, but upon God's mercy.") The fault of Augustine, later aggravated by Calvin, was that he traced the sovereignty of grace to the sovereignty of an inscrutable will, which was then absolutized and made the basis of a *double* predestination. But this absolute and inscrutable will is not the will of God as it is revealed in his act of grace in Christ. The Confession itself betrays the inconsistency when it counsels us in the final paragraph to attend to the will of God revealed in his word and so to be assured of our eternal election; for if there is another will of God, or another side to his will than that which is revealed in his word, we can hardly be expected to gain assurance of our election merely by closing our eyes to the alternative possibility of our rejection. If Christ is the authentic revelation of God, God has no other will than that which is revealed in him, and we may be fully assured that "he is able . . . to save them to the uttermost that come unto God by him." (Heb. 7:25.)

---

[3] Calvin virtually says this in so many words in his *Institutes*, Book I, Chapter XVI, Paragraph VIII (Allen's translation).

If the revelation of God in Christ makes it impossible for us to accept the proposition that God has foreordained some men to everlasting death "to the praise of his glorious justice," it does not follow that we must set up the alternative proposition that God has elected all men to salvation and will in fact save all, as some people have supposed. This matter will be discussed in connection with the final chapter of the Confession, which deals with the last judgment; but it may be said here that to set up either proposition is to confuse faith with logic; it is to abandon the position of the believer who trusts to the mercy of God extended to him in Christ ("Simply to Thy cross I cling") for that of the spectator who feels sufficiently sure of his own standing to indulge his curiosity regarding his neighbor. To all who would ask, "Lord, and what shall this man do?" the answer is, "What is that to thee? follow thou me." (John 21:21-22.)

chapter IV

OF CREATION

<hr>

CF IV, 1 It pleased God the Father, Son, and Holy Ghost, for the manifestation of the glory of his eternal power, wisdom, and goodness, in the beginning, to create or make of nothing the world, and all things therein, whether visible or invisible, in the space of six days, and all very good.

If the subject of revelation and of the Biblical testimony is "that knowledge of God, and of his will, which is necessary unto salvation" (CF I, 1), the question may be asked whether and how creation comes under that description. Is the knowledge of creation an essential ingredient of a saving knowledge of God? The question is not answered by pointing to the fact that creation is attested in the Bible, and in the opening pages at that; for this is not in itself sufficient to show how it is of vital interest to faith. As a matter of fact, references to creation are very infrequent in the Bible. So far as the Old Testament is concerned, the creation narratives are generally considered to be of relatively late composition, and it seems clear that the doctrine of creation played no vital part in the working faith of the people of Israel, at least before the Exile; if it was implicit in it from the beginning, it became explicit only in the faith of a prophetic minority. The infrequency with which creation is mentioned in the New Testament could be explained on the ground that the doctrine had become firmly established in Jewish faith by this time and could therefore be taken for granted, but at the same time it points up the question whether and how the doctrine is integral to the faith of the New Testament and the faith of the Christian church.

The answer to these questions is indicated in the opening words of Paragraph 1, "It pleased God the Father, Son, and Holy Ghost . . . to create . . . the world." This is a statement about God, rather than about the world. It is not so much creation we believe in, as rather God the Creator. The doctrine of creation is an element or aspect of faith in God. That is to say, faith has no independent interest in the fact that the world was created; the interest of faith is in affirming that the creation of the world is the work of God, and not of some postulated creator, but of the God of Christian faith, God the Father, Son, and Holy Spirit. The Biblical basis of this affirmation is found, not in the creation narratives of the Old Testament, but, as the Confession indicates, in those passages of the New Testament which ascribe to Christ a mediatorial role in creation as well as in salvation (John 1:2-3; Col. 1:15-16; Heb. 1:2; see also I Cor. 8:6). How the authors of these passages conceived of the mediatorial role of Christ in creation is a question which is very difficult to answer, but their interest did not lie in that direction. Their basic intention was to identify the Creator as the God and Father of Jesus Christ, and so to affirm the fundamental unity of creation and salvation in the eternal purpose of God, which he has revealed in Christ. (See Rom. 16:25-26.) The God who creates is none other than the God who saves, the God who was identified by the church as the triune God—Father, Son, and Holy Spirit; and the salvation of the world is the true end of its creation.

"for the manifestation of the glory of his eternal power, wisdom, and goodness." This is the answer to the question, Why did God create the world? The purpose of God in creation, as it is revealed in Christ, is the manifestation of his glory; and this, of course, is not vainglory, but the glory of his grace. (Eph. 1:6.) The same overflowing goodness, which is manifest in the salvation of the world, is also the ground of its existence. "For God is good, or rather he is in himself the source of goodness. Being good, he could not grudge anyone anything; therefore he did not grudge existence to any; and so he made all things out of nothing through his own Word, our Lord Jesus Christ."[1]

"in the beginning, to create or make of nothing." These phrases point to the unique character of creation as a work of God, and clearly mark the difference between the doctrine of creation and all theories concerning the origin of the world. There can be no conflict between Christian faith and scientific theory if this difference is properly understood. All attempts to account for the origin of the world on the basis of scientific inquiry can only presuppose creation; for science operates with the data of experience, and being created cannot be an object of experience, since it is the precondition of all our experience. Creation lies beyond the limits of human inquiry, at the point where faith apprehends God. Inquiry into origins is bound to seek them within existence, since the human mind cannot think the thought of any condition of existence which is without an antecedently existing condition. And thus, though scientific inquiry may succeed in tracing the existence of the world back to a condition, the antecedent condition of which cannot be ascertained, this is not creation. Creation signifies the absolute beginning of existence. The Biblical statement that "in the beginning God created" has been rendered in the formula, "creation out of nothing" (*creatio ex nihilo*), which is meant to distinguish it from any idea that God brought the world into existence by giving form to some previously existing but unformed matter, or, perhaps, that he generated it from the substance of his own being. Whenever we speak of any human artist or craftsman as creating, it is always in this sense; for no human being can create except he have some material to create with, whether it be sticks or stones or words or colors or tones. But when God created the world, he did not create it out of *something;* for before the world was brought into existence, there was *nothing,* i.e., nothing but God himself.

Creation out of nothing means that the precondition of ex-

---

[1] Athanasius, *De Incarnatione,* 3. From *The Early Christian Fathers,* translated by Henry Bettenson, p. 377. (Oxford University Press, 1956.)

istence is to be found nowhere in existence, but solely in the Creator himself. It is the positive aspect of the matter which receives the greater emphasis in the Bible, where it is expressed in terms of the divine word as the instrument or medium of creation. "God said, Let there be light: and there was light" (Gen. 1:3); "For he spake, and it was done; he commanded, and it stood fast" (Ps. 33:9). Creation by the word is implied in the Confession when it ascribes creation to the God who is Father, Son, and Holy Spirit; for the Son is identified with the word in the New Testament, in the passages cited above, and especially in John 1:1-14 where the main concern of the evangelist is to identify the word incarnate with the word by whom all things were made. The idea of the word or *logos* (which in Greek meant both the articulate word and the rational thought behind it) was used by many of the ancient Greeks to express the principle of intelligibility in reality; it was, they thought, because the world has a rational or meaningful structure that it can be understood. In the thought of the Bible, however, it is the existence of the world that is ascribed to the word. It is not some concept of pure being, discoverable by a process of intellectual abstraction, that underlies the existence of the world. The power of being is the creative word of God. "By the word of the LORD were the heavens made." (Ps. 33:6.) But this is not a discovery made by the analysis of existence. It is the answer of faith to the word revealed: "By faith we understand that the world was created by the word of God, so that what is seen was made out of things which do not appear." (Heb. 11:3, RSV.)

"the world, and all things therein, whether visible or invisible." The "world" is not here limited in sense to this planet which we inhabit, and it should not be supposed that the doctrine of creation in Biblical faith is bound up with such a view, as has sometimes been charged. It is true, of course, that the earth seemed bigger to the men of Biblical antiquity than it can to us in view of our vastly enlarged conceptions of the immensities of the astronomical universe. But though the earth was conceived as the center of creation in Biblical thought, it was never supposed to

constitute the whole of it. The creation narrative of Genesis 1
begins with the statement that "in the beginning God created
the heavens and the earth"; and the setting of the earth in its
larger context is an important element in what follows. The
"world" embraces both the heavens and the earth. This further
illustrates the distinctive character of the Biblical doctrine of
creation, which is anything but an attempt to explain the existence of the world. It reflects the recognition on the part of
Biblical man that the world in which he found himself placed has
two sides or two aspects: there is one aspect which is comprehen-
sible and manageable and in which he can feel at home; there is
another aspect which is incomprehensible and mysterious, and
before which he stands in awe and dread. The extension of our
knowledge of the world should not be allowed to blind us to how
much of the reality by which we are encompassed is still opaque.
Mystery surrounds us on every side. It is present in "the meanest
flower that blows." It looks at us from the eyes of every little
child. It encounters us in the depths of our own being; for we are
"fearfully and wonderfully made." (Ps. 139:14.) But there is more
than mystery. To the peoples of Biblical antiquity the "heavens"
stood also for the element of dread in the encompassing reality;
for they were regarded as the sphere of powers which exercise
sway over the lives of men and of nations. The existence of these
super-terrestrial arbiters of destiny is not denied in the Bible,
not even in the New Testament (see Col. 1:16; Eph. 6:12), but
Biblical faith affirms that they also are included in God's creation
and are subject to his power. This makes it doubly clear that faith
in creation is not a cosmogony, or attempt to explain the existence of the world; it is an act of supreme confidence in God
and a renunciation of all confidence in, and fear of, anything in
creation.

"in the space of six days." The "days" of the creation story in
Genesis 1 are manifestly not intended to be taken literally as
successive 24-hour periods, if for no other reason than that the
creation of the astronomical chronometers is represented in the
story as the work of the fourth "day." But it would be too prosaic

to ask what non-literal meaning is to be substituted for it. The broad truth which is expressed in this feature of the story is that God's creation is presented as a process extended over a period of time—a truth which would seem to be consistent with the evidence produced by the scientific study of origins. This is not to suggest that the Biblical author miraculously anticipated the theory of evolution. It is probable that he employed the idea of temporal sequence merely in order to enhance the principal feature in his picture of the created world, namely, that it is a place of order, in which everything is what it is, and, at the same time, is related to everything else. It is not how long God took to create the world that is of interest to faith, but that the world he created is a universe, a *cosmos*, an organized system. Faith in God the Creator is faith which in a manner embraces the world which he has created.

At the same time, however, the "six days" serve also to indicate that, while creation was spread over a space of time, it was actually completed within it: "Thus the heavens and the earth were finished, and all the host of them. And on the seventh day God ended his work which he had made; and he rested on the seventh day from all his work which he had made." (Gen. 2:1-2.) The six days of creation are followed by the seventh day of rest from the finished work of creation; and while the former may point to the continuation of the creative process, the latter points to its finality. The world, as God's finished work, is now possessed of a relative independence and structure of its own. It is indeed dependent on God's providential preservation, but its creation as such is finished. There is a real break between the Creator and the creation, a severance of the umbilical cord, so to speak; and this is necessary if there is to be a real relation between them.

"and all very good." The attitude of faith to creation and creaturely existence is fundamentally and consistently affirmative. There is a deep-rooted tendency in oriental thought to regard existence as evil and to seek deliverance from it as the supreme good. Some of the Greeks also inclined to the view that "Not to have been born is best of all" (Aeschylus), and throughout the history of western thought this pessimistic view has persisted among a minority; one of its twentieth-century spokesmen has said that "Existence is a disease of being." Against this, Biblical faith affirms that existence is fundamentally good. A creation of the divine goodness, attended with joy, it is itself a thing to be enjoyed. "Truly the light is sweet, and a pleasant thing it is for the eyes to behold the sun." (Eccl. 11:7.) The doctrine of creation is also consistently affirmative in its attitude toward existence, in contrast to the characteristic tendency of Greek thought to make a division in existence and to regard the material side as evil and only the non-material as good. Biblical faith affirms the goodness of matter as well as of spirit, of body as well as of soul. "Everything created by God is good" (I Tim. 4:4, RSV), and there is no inherent evil in matter as such.

It must be remembered, however, that in the story "very good" is the judgment of God himself on his creation. (Gen. 1:31.) It does not necessarily follow that the goodness of creation is manifest in the world as we know it now. The question of whether it has been affected by the ravages of sin will arise in our study of Chapter VI. In any case, "good" should not be interpreted here as pleasant. If creation is good in the eyes of God, it is because it is good for his purpose, not because it is designed to afford pleasure to us.

CF IV,2   After God had made all other creatures, he created man, male and female, with reasonable and immortal souls, endued with knowledge, righteousness, and true holiness after his own image, having the law of God written in their hearts, and power to fulfill it; and yet under a possibility of transgressing, being left to the liberty of their own will, which was subject unto change. Besides this law written in their hearts, they received a command not to eat of the tree of the knowledge of good and evil; which while they kept they were happy in their communion with God, and had dominion over the creatures.

The distinctive place of man in the scheme of creation is clearly indicated in the Genesis narratives: in chapter 1 the creation of man marks the climax of the six "days" (note how it is dramatically introduced by the divine act of deliberation, in contrast to the bare word of command previously employed—Gen. 1:26); in the second chapter the creation of man follows immediately the creation and irrigation of the earth and forms the center round which the rest of creation is organized. It is in and through man that God's purpose with creation is to be fulfilled (see Rom. 8:19-21); for the distinctive thing about man is that, while he belongs to creation—he is formed of the dust of the ground (Gen. 2:7)—he stands in a special relation to God: "God created man in his own image" (Gen. 1:27). This phrase has been variously interpreted. The obvious meaning would seem to be that man is like God, and if it be taken in this sense, the problem then is to determine where this likeness is to be seen. It has been thought that the writer of Genesis 1 saw the point of resemblance between man and God in man's upright stature, and in the Christian church the view was held for a long time that the image of God is located in man's reason. But there are two objections to attempts like these to identify the image of God with some element in the structure of man's being: (1) They are out of harmony with the dominant emphasis in the Biblical picture of man, which is on the difference, rather than the resemblance, between man as creature and God the Creator; God is incomparable (Isa. 40:18) and unimaginable (Exod. 20:4) in terms of anything that is to be found on earth, including man. (2) The New Testament speaks of man's re-creation in the image of God (Rom. 8:29; II Cor. 3:18; Col. 3:10), and this implies that the image of God has been lost or destroyed; but man has not lost his upright stature or his reason. A more satisfactory interpretation emerges if it is remembered that an image need not mean a replica or facsimile of an original; it can also mean an image in a mirror, and the peculiarity of this kind of image is that it subsists only in reflection from the original. (See James 1:23-24.) In this sense, the image of God points to a *correspondence,* rather than a resemblance, between man and God. It indicates that man is created for communion with God, and that this is not merely an option which he may exercise, but the basic structure of his being. As man is created for God, he cannot be himself by himself, but only in relation to God. He is created to be "visited" by God, and the answer to the question, What is man? can be found only in this context. (Ps. 8.) Man's essential being is a being-in-relation, or a being-in-reflection, or a being-in-response; he is himself when he answers the word of him in whose image he is created.

It is man's essential being or true nature which is defined in this paragraph. The question of whether it belongs to man as he actually exists, and as we know him today, will be considered in connection with Chapter VI. Here we are concerned with man's essential nature, or man as he truly is in accordance with the intention of his Creator. The detailed features, which are specified, are perhaps more intelligible if the picture be described in broad terms as that of a man who actually is what he is intended to be, or, in more abstract language, one whose existence conforms to his essence. His responsibility to God is realized in actual correspondence to God. Being free, he is subject to the law of God in the form of a positive command; but he has also "the law of God written in his heart." (See Rom. 2:15.) His freedom is his nature, his obligation his action, his imperative his indicative. And he is endowed with the capacity to be what he essentially is, in terms both of knowledge and power, or of reason and will.

"with reasonable and immortal souls." Man's reason or rational power was long regarded as a higher function of his soul (the lower being his life). The idea that the soul is immortal presents some difficulty; it cannot be securely founded on the passages of Scripture which are adduced in support of it; and if the term be taken in its strictly literal sense of "not liable to death," the idea would seem to be incompatible with the general tenor of Scripture, as it is expressed in the emphatic declaration that God alone has immortality. (I Tim. 6:16.) It is an unbiblical way of trying to express the great Biblical truth that God's purpose with man is not completed with his death; God has created man for an eternal destiny.

"being left to the liberty of their own will, which was subject unto change." The complex question of freedom and unfreedom is the special theme of Chapter XI and will be dealt with there. But it is worth noting here that the Confession evidently attempts to distinguish the freedom which belongs to man in his essential nature from a freedom of neutrality or indifference. It is a structured or oriented freedom, like the freedom of the compass needle to point to the magnetic north; man is free to be what he essentially is—which he is essentially in freedom. Should he choose to turn his will in another direction, like a compass needle which turns to the south, he is free to do so, but, having used this freedom, he is no longer free to be what he essentially is.

"male and female." Man's essential being involves, not only a relation to God, but also a relation to his fellow man. Man is not created to be an isolated, self-sufficient individual; for in the eyes of his Creator "it is not good that the man should be alone." (Gen. 2:18.) Man is essentially a social being. In the creation narratives in the Bible the social aspect of man's nature is focused in the relation between the sexes. The relation between male and female is the basis of the family, and the family in turn is the nucleus of the larger social unities to which man belongs.

"dominion over the creatures." The Biblical picture of man in his essential being is completed with this feature, which points to a third relation in which man is set, namely, his relation to the world around him. If man is set *under* God, and *beside* his fellow man, he is set *over* the world; he is given the authority and the power to use it in the service of his own needs and purposes. But this feature of man's being must not be isolated from its context. The point is not the magnitude of man's power, nor the extent of the subservience of the created world to him (which may seem questionable in view, say, of the nebula in Andromeda); it is that the exercise of his dominion over the world is one of the ways in which he has to be himself. For his essential being, created by God, is given to him as a task which he has to fulfill, in responsibility toward God, in association with his fellow man, and in the conquest of his environment. There is no support in the Bible for the romantic view that man's true being belongs to a "state of nature" and that civilization marks a progressive declension from it. On the contrary, the use of his God-given skills and energies to conquer nature and promote the advance of civilization is one essential element in his true being—one of the ways in which he has to be himself.

"which while they kept they were happy in their communion with God." The happiness of man in his essential being in responsive dependence on God contrasts with the condition of the man who has declared his independence of God and who knows only "the pursuit of happiness,"

> "And Joy, whose hand is ever at his lips
> Bidding adieu."[1]

---

[1] From "Ode on Melancholy" by John Keats.

▪ chapter V

OF PROVIDENCE

The word "providence" occurs only once in the Bible (King James Version), and there it is used for the administration of a Roman political official. (Acts 24:2. The same Greek word is used in Romans 13:14, where it is translated "provision.") It was first used of God's administration of the world in the Stoic philosophy, and it was imported from that source into the vocabulary of the Christian faith.

CF V,1   God, the great Creator of all things, doth uphold, direct, dispose, and govern all creatures, actions, and things, from the greatest even to the least, by his most wise and holy providence, according to his infallible foreknowledge, and the free and immutable counsel of his own will, to the praise of the glory of his wisdom, power, justice, goodness, and mercy.

The general theme of providence is the relation of God to his creation. It presupposes that the work of creation is finished, so that the creation stands over against the Creator with a relative but real independence. In creation God is the sole agent; he creates out of "nothing." But once the creation is finished, it is itself a source of activity, which has to be taken into account in the doctrine of providence. All the problems which arise in this field—and some of them are extremely difficult—are aspects of the basic problem of the relation between the action of God and the action of the creatures. If providence is to be distinguished from creation on the one side, it must also be distinguished from salvation on the other. This is of special importance in view of a tendency in the minds of some to look for the working out of God's final purpose with the world in this area. But God's providential dealings with the world are not definitive. God's final purpose with the world is its salvation, and his providential dealings with it are "provisional" or instrumental to that end. Providence is concerned with that aspect of God's relation to the world which is intermediate between its creation and its salvation.

God's providential dealings with his creation are here defined in the four verbs, "uphold, direct, dispose, and govern." The last three are virtually synonymous, and the four may therefore be taken to point to the two basic "modes" of God's providential work, as they are defined in the Shorter Catechism in the answer to Question 11: "God's works of providence are, his most holy, wise, and powerful preserving and governing all his creatures, and all their actions."

(1) In his providence God preserves his creatures; he upholds them in the existence which he has given them. The question of how he does it is the theme of Paragraph 3. The one thing which may be emphasized at this point is that God's providential preservation must be understood in terms of the nature of creaturely existence, which is finite or limited. We may not look to God's providence to preserve his creatures indefinitely; for that is not the kind of existence he has given them. Faith must be able to recognize the hand of providence in the termination of creaturely existence, and to say, with Job, "The LORD gave, and the LORD hath taken away; blessed be the name of the LORD." (Job 1:21.)

(2) In his providence God governs his creatures. The basic thought here is not that of rule or control—though it, of course, is included—but is that of direction toward a goal or purpose. A "governor" was originally a steersman or pilot (as in James 3:4, KJV). In his providential government of his creation God controls its course in such a way as to direct it toward the purpose of his will—a purpose which may lie beyond the scope of his providential dealings with it. The phrases which complete the first paragraph are intended to emphasize that the plan and the purpose of God's providence are determined by himself alone.

CF V,2   Although in relation to the foreknowledge and decree of God, the first cause, all things come to pass immutably and infallibly, yet, by the same providence, he
ordereth them to fall out according to the nature of second causes, either necessarily, freely, or contingently.

The sovereign control of God over all that comes to pass does
not mean that he is the sole agent. God is the sole agent in creation, as was said above, but in providence the activity of the
creatures is a factor which has to be taken into account. This
paragraph asserts that God's providential activity not only
includes the activity of the creatures but detracts in no way from
the integrity and diversity of their activity. The creatures do not
become puppets in the hands of an almighty manipulator; they
continue to act, and to act in their own distinctive ways. The
Confession distinguishes three modes of activity or operation
which may be observed in the course of events. There are things
which come to pass "necessarily"; their occurrence is necessitated
by other occurrences. The reference is to what are commonly
called the laws of nature. Those patterns of regularity which are
to be observed in so much that takes place in the world, and
which have at times been thought to leave no room for providence, are cited here as a providential arrangement, as, indeed,
they may well be, when it is considered how vastly they facilitate
our dealings with the world. The things which come to pass
"freely" are those which originate in the free decisions of animate
wills, human or otherwise. The things which come to pass "contingently" are those which are the product neither of some
pattern of necessity nor of some free decision, but which can
only be ascribed to "chance." Chance often lies in the borderland,
where necessity and freedom meet, as with the priest who went
down the Jericho road in the parable (Luke 10:31); but it differs
from each of them. Things happen in these three different ways
in the world, and yet their happening is under the sovereign
control of God's providence. How can this be understood? The
Confession presents it in terms of two different causalities: God

in his providential activity is "the first cause," and the creatures in their diverse modes of operation are called "second causes"; everything that comes to pass is the effect of this dual causality, in which God acts first and the creatures second.

The propriety of applying the concept of causality to the activity of God has been questioned by some who have taken the view that causality operates only within the created order and cannot be applied to God without a virtual denial of his transcendence. It is true that if causality be limited to the sense of physical or mechanical causality, like the action of steam on a piston, it could not be applied to God. But it is clear that the notion is used in the Confession in a very broad sense, as may be gathered from the diverse modes of operation which are grouped under the heading of second causes, and that the relation of first and second causes is not conceived as that of two forces operating in the same field. Since the first cause is itself the cause of the causality of the second causes (like hand and pen in writing, to cite the favorite illustration), the concept of cause is used analogically; and there seems no reason why it should not be, so long as this is borne in mind. The way in which creaturely activity causes things to come to pass (and this is mysterious enough) is *like* (not identical with) the way in which the providential activity of God "causes" his creatures to act.

CF V,3   God, in his ordinary providence, maketh use of means, yet is free to work without, above, and against them, at his pleasure.

The distinction is made here between the ordinary and the extraordinary workings of God's providence. Ordinarily God conducts his providential works through the means of his creatures; he employs them as his instruments, and his activity is mediated through theirs. The best illustration of the instrumental or mediate role which the creatures themselves play in God's providential preservation and government of them is seen in the family. And since the mutual support and direction of the members of the family are also the functions of the broader political and economic organizations of human society, they too are instruments of divine providence: "the authorities are ministers of God." (Rom. 13:6, RSV.)

But God is also "free to work without, above, and against" means, "at his pleasure." The reference is to miracles. If miracles are looked at, as they have often been, as extraordinary events, i.e., events which fall outside the normal order of providence, they tend to take on the appearance of arbitrary interferences with that order; and then the question arises, If God has established the providential order, why should he interfere with it? This question is partially answered by the appeal to the "freedom" of God to override the providential order "at his pleasure." But while God is indeed free in the sense that he is not bound by the providential order which he has established, his exercise of this freedom is not arbitrary or capricious, as the language of the Confession might suggest. The freedom of God is his freedom to pursue his saving purpose, and this, as was noted above, goes beyond the purpose of providence, which is instrumental to it. The miracles of the New Testament, and above all the miracles of the Incarnation and the Resurrection, supremely illustrate this. They are events which occur in the world; and from the perspective of the ordinary working of God's providence, by which the world is governed, they may look like interferences with that order. But they are really acts of salvation, and their meaning is to be found in the purpose they serve. They are manifestations of "the powers of the world to come" (Heb. 6:5) at work within this world.

CF V,4   The almighty power, unsearchable wisdom, and infinite goodness of God, so far manifest themselves in his providence, that it extendeth itself even to the first fall, and all other sins of angels and men, and that not by a bare permission, but such as hath joined with it a most wise and powerful bounding, and otherwise ordering and governing of them, in a manifold dispen-

sation, to his own holy ends; yet so, as the sinfulness
thereof proceedeth only from the creature, and not
from God; who being most holy and righteous, neither
is nor can be the author or approver of sin.

The theme of this paragraph is the relation of God's providence
to sin. Since this is a sinful world, and the general theme of the
doctrine of providence is God's relation to it, it could be argued
that the Confession should have dealt with sin before providence.
In placing providence before sin the Confession indirectly attests
the truth asserted in this paragraph—that providence is superior
to sin. Sin is contrary to the will of God, but it is not outside the
control of his will. Though its presence in creation is no part of
God's purpose, this does not mean that he was helpless to prevent it. Sin exists by his "permission." It is an implicate of the
freedom of will with which he endowed his human creatures;
it is a risk which he took when he created them "under a possibility of transgressing" his law. (CF IV, 2.) But though the possibility may be said to be of God's creation, the actuality is not;
nor does he approve of it, for sin is an abuse of freedom.

God's providential control over sin is seen in the fact that
though it exists by his permission, it is "not by a bare permission."
The permission is coupled with a "bounding" and a "governing";
God sets bounds to the possibility of sin, and at the same time he
can press it into the service of his will. There are limits to the
evil men can accomplish (though they may sometimes be hard
to discern), because evil is essentially parasitical, it thrives only
by preying on the body of good, like disease; and by the same
token, it is essentially destructive, and its destructive propensity is
apt to terminate in self-destruction. And though sin is contrary
to God's purpose, he is able to make it the instrument of his purpose, and so to bring good out of evil. The classic examples of
this in Biblical history are the betrayal of Jesus by Judas, which
was "according to the definite plan and foreknowledge of God"
(Acts 2:23, RSV), and its Old Testament prototype, the betrayal of
Joseph by his brethren: they "thought evil" against him; "but

God meant it unto good, to bring to pass, as it is this day, to save much people alive" (Gen. 50:20).

CF V,5   The most wise, righteous, and gracious God, doth oftentimes leave for a season his own children to manifold temptations and the corruption of their own hearts, to chastise them for their former sins, or to discover unto them the hidden strength of corruption and deceitfulness of their hearts, that they be humbled; and to raise them to a more close and constant dependence for their support upon himself, and to make them more watchful against all future occasions of sin, and for sundry other just and holy ends.

The substance of this paragraph is that faith in providence is not easy. It is a matter of faith, not of sight, and, as such, it has often to be exercised in a world from which the hand of providence seems far removed. Faith in providence is not the key to a secure and comfortable life; it is more like entering a school, in which we must learn through a stern and sometimes painful discipline what it means to walk by this faith. It is a faith which is exposed to "manifold temptations."

It may be remarked that neither here, nor in the preceding paragraph which treats of the place of sin under God's providence, is there any explicit reference to "the problem of evil" as it is commonly understood today. It has come to be felt by many that the hardest problem with which faith in providence has to wrestle is not sin, the evil which originates in the sinful wills of men, but *natural* evil, the evil which comes from natural sources, such as cancer, earthquake, tornado, and the like. Perhaps such things are implied in the "manifold temptations" (or "trials," in the broader sense of the New Testament term), to which the children of God are exposed; but, if so, the Confession has no interest in them except as they serve as occasions of sin or as instruments of God's providential discipline. It regards the sufferings of men as important only for the bearing they have on their relation to God. The triumph of faith in the acceptance of suffering is probably the best solution that can be found to the problem of evil.

CF V,6   As for those wicked and ungodly men whom God,
as a righteous judge, for former sins, doth blind and
harden; from them he not only withholdeth his grace,
whereby they might have been enlightened in their
understandings, and wrought upon in their hearts;
but sometimes also withdraweth the gifts which they
had; and exposeth them to such objects as their corruption makes occasion of sin; and withal, giveth them
over to their own lusts, the temptations of the world,
and the power of Satan; whereby it cometh to pass that
they harden themselves, even under those means which
God useth for the softening of others.

This paragraph deals with the difficult case of those who are
unresponsive to God's providential discipline and who become
so confirmed in their sinful ways that it produces in them an
effect opposite to that described in Paragraph 5. It is an index of
the reality of the freedom with which God has endowed men,
that when they misuse their freedom to choose sin, they are free
to reap the extreme consequence of their choice, which consists
in their complete enslavement to sin (John 8:34; Rom. 6:16);
their minds and hearts and wills may be so completely dominated
by sin that every move they make involves them more deeply in
its power. But it is also an index of the superiority of God's
providential control over human freedom, that even when men
reach the condition of "abandoned sinners," it is God who has
abandoned them. (Rom. 1:24, 26, 28.)

God is said to abandon such men to "the power of Satan."
The name of Satan is introduced here for the first time, and
quite casually; neither here nor anywhere else is any attempt
made to explain who or what Satan is. The silence of the Confession is wiser than the zeal of those who would fain make "belief in a personal devil" into a test of orthodoxy. Orthodoxy is
ill served by such zeal; for the devil cannot be an object of Christian belief in the same way as God; he is not so represented in

any of the Creeds. We believe in God because he has revealed himself; but we have not been favored with a revelation of the devil. On the contrary, it is the genius of the devil to remain un-revealed; and, as it has been said, "The devil's cleverest wile is to persuade us that he does not exist." (Beaudelaire.) The Confession is interested only in the function of Satan, and it makes the paradoxical assertion that though the function of Satan is in opposition to God, it is at the same time under God's providential control. As Luther said, the devil is "God's devil." But this must be understood "eschatologically." It should not be taken to minimize the magnitude or gravity of evil; it is an expression of the assurance of faith in the ultimate triumph of God over all that opposes him.

CF V,7   As the providence of God doth, in general, reach to all creatures; so, after a most special manner, it taketh care of his church, and disposeth all things to the good thereof.

The distinction between God's general providence which embraces all his creatures (i.e., everything that he has created), and his most special providence which applies to the church only, has sometimes been enlarged by the inclusion of an intermediate degree, special providence (as distinct from *most* special), which was held to apply to his rational creatures, i.e., men. The idea of distinctions of degree in God's providence presents some difficulty. If it means that God takes more care of men than he does of things, and most care of the church, faith would be hard to reconcile with experience. It would certainly be dangerous to encourage members of the church to believe that they have a special title to protection against the slings and arrows of outrageous fortune. It is probable that here, as in Paragraph 3, the Confession is using the doctrine of providence to express a truth which really lies outside the scope of this doctrine. The church certainly holds a special place in the purpose of God—it is the primary object and the organ of his salvation for the whole world —but this place is not necessarily to be construed in terms of special providence, in the sense of special protection. The promise of perpetuity to the church is related to its special vocation (Matt. 16:18); and fidelity to its vocation on the part of the church may result in its being more exposed than the rest of the world to the hardships and hazards of the providential order. This is what Paul found (II Cor. 11:23-29); and if he was able to triumph over his afflictions, it was because he looked beyond God's providence to his eternal purpose in Jesus Christ (II Cor. 4:8-11; 6:3-10; and especially Rom. 8:28).

▪ chapter VI

OF THE FALL OF MAN, OF SIN,
AND OF THE PUNISHMENT THEREOF

CF VI,1   Our first parents, being seduced by the subtilty and temptation of Satan, sinned in eating the forbidden fruit. This their sin God was pleased, according to his wise and holy counsel, to permit, having purposed to order it to his own glory.

It was stated in CF IV, 2, that, while men were created to conform to the will of their Creator, they were "left to the liberty of their own will," and so "under a possibility of transgressing." This chapter deals with the realization of this possibility, in sin and its dire consequences.

The first sentence of Paragraph 1 summarizes the narrative of Genesis 3, which should be read as a *description* of how sin came into the world, not an *explanation*. The existence of sin in man cannot be explained by referring to the serpent; for this would only raise the anterior question concerning the existence of sin in the serpent. An explanation of sin is in principle impossible; for to explain a thing means to establish its place in the general scheme of things, and sin has no place in the created scheme of things. It is the thing which has fundamentally no right to exist. The figure of the serpent, which is here identified with the devil in accordance with Revelation 12:9 and 20:2, is a symbol of the inexplicability of sin. At the same time, however, it is an index of the fact that sin does not originate in man, and, therefore, cannot be ascribed to some propensity in the physical element of his nature. Sensuality is a consequence of sin, as is shown in Paragraph 2, not the origin of it. The origin of sin, so far as man is concerned, is temptation; i.e., it is suggested to him from a source which is not in himself. Man sins when he responds to temptation. And if it be asked how man comes to respond to temptation, the answer must be given, not in terms of his "lower" nature, but in terms of his "highest" gift of freedom; for in the Biblical narrative the inducement consists of a proffered enhancement of his freedom: he is offered the chance to exchange his freedom *for* God for freedom *from* God, by substituting his self-chosen end for his prescribed end, and so transgressing the line which separates him from God, and becoming himself "like God." (Gen. 3:5, RSV.) This is what Augustine meant when he said that the essence of sin is pride. Man is tempted to raise himself above himself, and so doing he precipitates his fall. (For God's permission of sin see treatment of CF V, 4.)

CF VI,2   By this sin they fell from their original righteousness and communion with God, and so became dead in sin, and wholly defiled in all the faculties and parts of soul and body.

The consequence of sin in man is the loss of his essential being, as it is defined in CF IV, 2 in terms of communion with God and dominion over the world. The Confession omits reference to the effects of sin on his relation to his fellow men and on his relation to the world (though its effect on the latter is obliquely implied in the final phrase of CF IV, 2), and concentrates on the loss of his communion with God and its concomitant effects on his own nature. Having yielded to temptation and chosen freedom from God, sinful man obtains what he chose. The bond which bound him to God is severed; he becomes separated from God; his life is now a life in the absence of God. By the same token he loses his own essential being and becomes divided against himself. What he *is* contradicts what he ought to be, and this contradiction makes his life a living death. His nature becomes de-natured, and the effects extend throughout the entire range of his being; he becomes "wholly defiled in all the faculties and parts of soul and body."

The strong language in which the effects of sin on man's nature are depicted here has to be understood in the light of the Roman Catholic doctrine to which it is opposed. According to the Roman Catholic doctrine, the fall of man involved only the loss of his "original righteousness," which is understood as a kind of supernatural endowment, and the nature of man was relatively unaffected by it. The Reformers rejected this doctrine on the basis of the message of the New Testament, which is not that man is only partially in need of salvation. They felt that since man is wholly in need of salvation, his condition must be one of "total depravity"; but in depicting this condition they sometimes used language which seemed to suggest that every vestige of good in man had been destroyed by sin and that man had virtually ceased to be a man and had become a monster. Such a picture of human depravity has been an object of resentment, and understandably so, for it is manifestly overdrawn. It rests on a false antithesis to the Roman Catholic view. The true antithesis to the Roman Catholic view that only part of man's being is affected by the ravages of sin is that there is no part of man's being which is not affected by them, not that every part and function of his being has become completely sinful. Complete sinfulness, or "pure evil," represents the condition of Satan, and for man to have attained it would mean that he had ceased to be human and become Satanic. But, while this condition may be attainable in marginal cases, the real tragedy and pathos of the condition of sinful man is that he becomes a battlefield of *good and evil,* a being torn by conflicting impulses and divided against himself. Were man so wholly overrun by the forces of sin that every aspiration or impulse of good in him was crushed, this would really be an easement of his condition. It is, as Paul found, the inner conflict, due to the presence of warring forces within him, which constitutes his "death in sin" and elicits from him the anguished cry, "Wretched man that I am! Who will deliver me from this body of death?" (Rom. 7:24, rsv.)

CF VI,3   They being the root of all mankind, the guilt of this
sin was imputed, and the same death in sin and corrupted nature conveyed to all their posterity, descending from them by ordinary generation.

This paragraph presents a brief but carefully worded statement
of the doctrine of "original sin." A close study of its terms may
help to remove some of the popular misconceptions which sur-
round this doctrine. The doctrine has been popularly supposed to
mean that we inherit the guilt of the sin of our first parents,
simply because we are their lineal descendants, and also, perhaps,
because there is something inherently sinful about the manner
in which we are brought into existence. Since it is manifestly un-
reasonable that one individual should be saddled with the guilt
of another for an act committed far away and long ago, just because the man who committed the act was his ancestor (and there
might be some question about this), some have been disposed to
reject the doctrine altogether. In order to understand the doctrine aright, it is advisable to attend first to the basic truth or
truths with which it is concerned. The basic truth is our solidarity
in sin. We are not isolated individuals, either in our sinning or in
anything else we do. As "none of us lives to himself, and none of
us dies to himself" (Rom. 14:7, RSV), so none of us sins to himself.
Sin is not something we commit only by our individual acts; it is
something in which we are involved together. We are not only
sinners; we are also co-sinners. The Confession bases the truth of
our solidarity in sin on the unity of mankind, but it presents the
latter in two different ways, which must be carefully distinguished.

"They being the root of all mankind." Since the reference is
to our first parents, and since the idea of our descent from them
is perfectly intelligible, it may seem strange that the Confession
should have recourse to a metaphor and speak of them as the
"root." The reason is that the Confession is pointing to the fact
that our relation to our first parents is not only one of descent;
we also stand in an organic relation to them, like that of the tree

to its root. We are not only *from* Adam, we are also *in* Adam (I Cor. 15:22); Adam is the representative or head of sinful humanity, which is unified *in* him, just as the new humanity has its unifying head and center *in* Christ, in whom it abides like branches in the vine (John 15:1-8). It is because Adam fills this representative role in relation to mankind that he forms the counterpart of Christ, "a type of the one who was to come." (Rom. 5:14, RSV.) And, most important of all, it is to this relationship that the Confession relates our solidarity in guilt. Guilt is not transmitted by heredity; it is *imputed,* i.e., it is ascribed to us in a legal or moral way, in virtue of our involvement in the common sin of mankind. We all belong together, and we are all together responsible for the sin of all.

The other relationship in which we stand to our first parents, by way of descent or heredity, is named second, because in the context of this doctrine it is consequential on the first. What is *conveyed* to us from our first parents through this channel and what we receive from them by inheritance is, not the guilt of their sin, which cannot be inherited, but "the same death in sin and corrupted nature" which is the consequence of sin. (Compare Par. 2.) The corruption of our nature, which we derive from our heredity, is not itself sin, but it constitutes a predisposition or bias toward sin which becomes apparent as soon as we are exposed to temptation.

It may be added that by placing the imputation of guilt before the transmission of corruption the Confession makes it clear that the truth of the doctrine of original sin does not depend on the possibility of identifying the sinners who were the "first parents" or the "root" of all mankind. Our common involvement in the circle of sinful humanity stands, even if we cannot locate the center of the circle, and it is not necessary that we should be able to trace our ancestry to its source in order to establish the fact that we are subject to the influence of heredity.

"descending from them by ordinary generation." This qualification attached to the posterity who are affected by original sin is intended to exclude Christ, who, though he was "the son of

Adam" (Luke 3:38), could not be said to be descended from him by *ordinary* generation, if he was born of a virgin. But the idea that Jesus was exempted from the guilt and corruption of original sin by being born of a virgin would seem to imply that the transmission of original sin is bound up in some way with the normal sexual union of male and female in procreation. This idea is one of those "doctrines of men" to which the Confession refers in I, 10, and which will be found, on examination, to have no foundation in the New Testament. Matthew and Luke record that Jesus was born of a virgin, but neither by them nor by any other writer in the New Testament is virgin birth adduced as ground of his divinity or his sinlessness.

CF VI,4   From this original corruption, whereby we are utterly indisposed, disabled, and made opposite to all good, and wholly inclined to all evil, do proceed all actual transgressions.

This paragraph relates to the hereditary aspect of our involvement in original sin, and it is open to the same criticism as Paragraph 2. There can, indeed, be no quarrel with the basic truth to which the paragraph points, namely, that we inherit with our nature a disposition or bias toward sin which pre-conditions our actual sins. In this sense it is true (as it has been put) that sin precedes sins. But there are two objections to the manner in which this truth is formulated in the Confession. In the first place, the corruption of our nature is here represented as the *source* of our actual sins in such a one-sided way as to undercut our guilt. The distinction between the guilt of sin and the attendant corruption, which is drawn in the preceding paragraph, appears to be forgotten, and our guilt is here derived from our corruption. Our corruption is a pre-condition of our actual sins, but if we are completely determined by it, it cannot be the source of their guilt. In the second place, the description of our corruption in terms of total aversion to good and total addiction to evil is exaggerated, and is, in fact, contradicted in CF XVIII, 7, where it is stated that unregenerate men are capable of some good. The corruption of sinful man is not that he is "utterly indisposed, disabled, and made opposite to all good," for such a condition would be Satanic, but that he is incapable of any good which is not, in some degree, infected with evil.

CF VI,5   This corruption of nature, during this life, doth remain in those that are regenerated: and although it be through Christ pardoned and mortified, yet both itself, and all the motions thereof, are truly and properly sin.

This paragraph anticipates a point which belongs to a later context and is fully intelligible only in the light of the doctrines of justification and sanctification (Chapters XIII and XV). The point is that while sinners receive through Christ full release from the guilt of sin (justification), their deliverance from corruption of nature is partial and incomplete (sanctification), and on that account they continue to be sinners, although at the same time they are justified. Further, since this condition persists so long as they live, the attainment of a state of sinless perfection within this present life is impossible.

CF VI,6   Every sin, both original and actual, being a transgression of the righteous law of God, and contrary thereunto, doth, in its own nature, bring guilt upon the sinner, whereby he is bound over to the wrath of God, and curse of the law, and so made subject to death, with all miseries spiritual, temporal, and eternal.

In this final paragraph the Confession returns to the consequences of sin which were mentioned before in Paragraph 2. The intention here is to assert their intrinsic character; that is to say, they are not attached to it in an arbitrary way, as a fine is attached to a crime; they are consequences which sin involves "in its own nature"; it is because of the kind of thing sin is that it brings them. The paragraph is best understood if it is read in the light of the statement of the essential being of man in CF

IV, 2. It can then be seen that the consequences of sin affect the main elements which belong to the essential being of man according to the intention of his Creator. They may be summarized as loss of communion with God, loss of conformity to his law, loss of life, and loss of happiness. By his sin man loses his communion with God, but he does not thereby sever his relation to God; it is changed into a relation of alienation, in which man in his guilt stands over against God in his wrath. By sin man loses that natural conformity to the law which would make his obedience spontaneous, but he does not escape the law. The law now becomes his accuser and judge, convicting him of his non-conformity to it and pronouncing the sentence of his doom. Intended to minister to man's life, it proves to be death to him. (Rom. 7:10; II Cor. 3:6-7.) And so man becomes "subject to death," not in the sense that he acquires mortality, but in the sense that his life, now alienated from the source of his life, becomes a life-unto-death and so, in effect, a living death. Finally, sinful man experiences the loss of happiness; for he knows that he must end in death before he can attain the end of his life, and the constant striving to overcome the frustration of such a life-compounded-with-death fills him with care and anxiety. It is the fear of missing his end that is the source of all man's misery—a misery which is endless.

◼ chapter VII

OF GOD'S COVENANT WITH MAN

CF VII,1   The distance between God and the creature is so great, that although reasonable creatures do owe obedience unto him as their Creator, yet they could never have any fruition of him, as their blessedness and reward, but by some voluntary condescension on God's part, which he hath been pleased to express by way of covenant.

The use of the idea of the covenant as the framework of God's dealings with men is a feature of the Reformed theological tradition and, more especially, of a movement within that tradition, which became active in the middle of the seventeenth century and which employed the idea so extensively that it came to be known as the Federal theology (*foedus* being the Latin for covenant). In view of the central part which it plays in the Bible —even in the titles of its two main divisions, which are called "The Old Covenant" and "The New Covenant"—it may seem strange that the idea should ever have been neglected. The reason is that in the theology of the pre-Reformation church the prevailing tendency for many centuries had been to construe the relations and the dealings between God and men in impersonal, or sub-personal, categories, such as substance; witness, especially, the Roman Catholic doctrine of the sacraments. It was the realization that such categories are inadequate to the purpose, and that they must be replaced by categories of personal relationship, which led to the revival of interest in the idea of the covenant among the Reformers of the sixteenth century. Calvin made use of it in discussing the relation between the Old Testament and the New. (*Institutes,* Book II, Chapters IX-XI; compare Paragraphs 5 and 6 of this chapter.) The Westminster Confession of Faith is considered to reflect the influence of the Federal theology of the following century, the principal architect of which was a Dutch theologian, named Cocceius; it is the first Confession to devote a special chapter to the topic.

A covenant is a compact or agreement between two parties in which they bind themselves to each other in a relationship involving mutual obligations. Biblical examples are the covenant between Abraham and Abimelech, which was equivalent to a "non-aggression pact" (Gen. 21:22-32), and the covenant between David and Jonathan, which was like a compact of friendship (I Sam. 18:3). Ordinarily such convenants are made between equals; and it is for this reason, as the Confession states, that the use of the covenant in the context of the relations between God and man, where that condition does not obtain, is possible only in virtue of "some voluntary condescension on God's part." Man is said to be under obligation to God in virtue of the ontological relation between the creature and the Creator; but God is not bound to man, except as he freely chooses to enter into such a relation to him. That he does so "by way of covenant" is an act of grace; the adoption by God of this human relationship as the form of his relation to men is an expression of the same grace by which, in the fullness of time, he took our flesh upon him, and in it did his decisive deed for the salvation of the world. Indeed, it is in the light of the covenant that the true dimensions of grace can be seen, for the grace of God is not (as it has sometimes been represented) a kind of capricious freedom in which he condescends to man at unpredictable moments; it is a freedom in which he binds himself to man in a structured relationship, within which he is really accessible to man: "I . . . will be your God, and ye shall be my people." (Lev. 26:12.) By his grace the people of his covenant can not only seek him but have him.

CF VII,2   The first covenant made with man was a covenant
of works, wherein life was promised to Adam, and in
him to his posterity, upon condition of perfect and
personal obedience.

The notion of a covenant of works is one of the more controversial elements of the Federal theology. It is not expressly stated
in Scripture that God made such a covenant with Adam; and
the idea has only a tenuous foundation in the passages adduced
in support of it, such as Genesis 2:17. Moreover, it is not clear
in what respect the covenant of works differs from the relation
between the Creator and the creature which is referred to at the
beginning of the previous paragraph, and which is said to bring
the creature under obligation of obedience without any covenant.
Some of the Federal theologians preferred to speak of a covenant
of nature as the framework of the creature's obligation, including
Adam in it as well; and this appears to be the meaning of the
Confession when it treats of the closely related problem of the
law of God in Chapter XXI; for it there identifies the moral
law, which is binding upon all men (Par. 5), with the law which
God gave to Adam as a covenant of works (Par. 1). The covenant
of works, or the covenant of nature, seemed to be logically de-
manded as the pre-condition of the covenant of grace, which
forms the central theme of the Biblical revelation; but in spite
of the difficulties it presents, it indirectly attests an important
truth, namely, that the relation between God and man cannot be
construed as an abstract metaphysical problem, but only in terms
of the specific relationship which God in his grace has established with man.

CF VII,3   Man, by his fall, having made himself incapable of
life by that covenant, the Lord was pleased to make a
second, commonly called the covenant of grace: wherein
he freely offered unto sinners life and salvation by
Jesus Christ, requiring of them faith in him, that they
may be saved, and promising to give unto all those
that are ordained unto life, his Holy Spirit, to make
them willing and able to believe.

CF VII,4   This covenant of grace is frequently set forth in
the Scripture by the name of a testament, in reference
to the death of Jesus Christ, the testator, and to the
everlasting inheritance, with all things belonging to it,
therein bequeathed.

The principal theme of this chapter, which is now introduced,
is God's covenant-relation with *fallen* man—and this is the
principal theme of the Confession as a whole. When it is introduced as *"commonly called* the covenant of grace," this may be
intended to indicate that the name is not itself Biblical, but was
actually coined in the Federal theology; it may also refer to the
fact, stated in Paragraph 1, that it is an act of grace on God's part
to enter into any kind of covenant relation with man. God does
not begin to be gracious when he makes the covenant of grace,
as it is called; but it is now that the full depth of his grace, which
is present in all his dealings with man, comes to light. The
covenant of works, if such there was, was made with unfallen
man; but this man nowhere exists. The only man we know is
fallen man, the man who by his sin has alienated himself from
God and has lost God. But though this man has lost God, God
does not lose hold of him; God's purpose to bring man into
communion with himself and into conformity to his will stands
firm in spite of man's defection, and in his grace he extends his
hand and freely offers to sinners "life and salvation by Jesus
Christ." The covenant of grace forms the framework of the great
truth which lives at the heart of the gospel, that nothing can defeat God's "love for man" (Titus 3:4, literally translated), which is
grounded in his eternal purpose, and "if we are faithless, he
remains faithful—for he cannot deny himself" (II Tim. 2:13, RSV).

The point referred to in Paragraph 4 is largely linguistic. It
well illustrates the risks involved in translation from one language to another and points to the importance of reference to the
original language of Scripture, as stated in CF I, 8. In the English
Bible (King James Version) the word "testament" is frequently
employed in the sense of "covenant," and could well be replaced
by it, as it is in most modern translations, in all but two passages.

The Hebrew word for covenant in the Old Testament had only this one sense, but the word which was employed to render it in the Greek translation of the Old Testament, and which was later taken up in the New, had another meaning (it was, in fact, its primary meaning), namely, a will. In Latin this became *testamentum* and passed into English as testament, which, of course, has no other meaning than will (in ordinary speech). Its use as the rendering of covenant is confusing to the English reader, but it was probably adopted because there are two passages in the New Testament where play is made with the double meaning of the Greek word (*diatheke*). In Galatians 3 and Hebrews 9, where the theme is the covenant of grace, the other meaning of the term (i.e., testament or will) is invoked in order to bring out the necessity of the death of Christ, since the death of the testator is necessary in order to put the will into effect, and also in order to point to the eschatological aspect of the Christian salvation, which is often presented in the New Testament under the figure of an inheritance (e.g., Heb. 9:15).

The meaning and terms of the covenant of grace will be considered in full detail as they are developed in the course of the following chapters.

CF VII,5   This covenant was differently administered in the time of the law, and in the time of the gospel: under the law it was administered by promises, prophecies, sacrifices, circumcision, the paschal lamb, and other types and ordinances delivered to the people of the Jews, all fore-signifying Christ to come, which were for that time sufficient and efficacious, through the operation of the Spirit, to instruct and build up the elect in faith in the promised Messiah, by whom they had full remission of sins, and eternal salvation; and is called the Old Testament.

CF VII,6   Under the gospel, when Christ the substance was exhibited, the ordinances in which this covenant is dispensed, are the preaching of the word, and the ad-

ministration of the sacraments of baptism and the
Lord's supper; which, though fewer in number, and
administered with more simplicity and less outward
glory, yet in them it is held forth in more fullness,
evidence, and spiritual efficacy, to all nations, both
Jews and Gentiles; and is called the New Testament.
There are not, therefore, two covenants of grace dif-
fering in substance, but one and the same under various dispensations.

The distinction which is drawn in these paragraphs must itself
be carefully distinguished from the distinction which is drawn
in the Bible between "the old covenant" and "the new covenant"
and which is embodied in the titles of its two component parts.
The Confession comprises both the old and new covenants within
the one covenant of grace, and reduces the distinction between
them to a difference in the modes in which this one covenant was
administered at different times. They would then be more appropriately described as different dispensations. The Confession
places them at different times, the time of the law and the time
of the gospel, and it indicates some of the principal ways in which
they differ and which have respect to their complexity, their
constituency, and their orientation. But more important than all
the differences between them is the underlying identity of the
covenant which is dispensed with equal efficacy in the forms of
both law and gospel. This affirmation of identity in diversity
reflects the teaching of the New Testament, and especially that
of Paul on the complex relation between the law and the gospel.
Sometimes Paul makes a point of the contrast between the law
and the gospel, almost as if the publication of the gospel involved
the abrogation of the law. (See Gal. 2:11-21.) But nearly always
he is careful to add that though there is a sense in which the
gospel sets aside the law, there is a sense in which it fulfills it
(see Gal. 3:21-24; Rom. 3:21); for the law points forward to
Christ and leads us to him, and so it may be said to have the
gospel hidden within it, much as the tables of the law were them-

selves hidden in the ark of the covenant (Deut. 31:26). The true meaning of the law is to be found in its original intention as a dispensation of the covenant of grace, "fore-signifying Christ to come," and this meaning is fulfilled in the gospel. But the gospel is opposed to what had become of the law in the synagogue of the Jews, where it had been construed legalistically as a "covenant of works," and where its true evangelical meaning had been lost to sight, because, as Paul says, "a veil lies over their minds." (II Cor. 3:15, RSV.)

It may be added that in describing those to whom the covenant of grace was dispensed in the forms of the law as "the people of the Jews," the Confession is using this name in the broad sense as equivalent to the people of Israel. Strictly, however, the name is applicable only to the people of Judah after the disruption of the kingdom, who in New Testament times were represented by the Jews of the synagogue. Since it was among them that the law had been distorted from its original intention, it would have been better if the name had not been used in this place.

The distinctive features of the dispensation of the covenant under the law are said to be the complexity of the apparatus employed, its restriction to one people, and its prospective orientation; the distinctive features of the dispensation "under the gospel, when Christ the substance was exhibited," are said to be the simplicity of the apparatus, its increased efficacy, and its extension to all nations. If it is implied that the relative simplicity of the forms of dispensation under the gospel is a consequence of the exhibition of the substance, this is dangerous, since it seems to play into the hands of some sects in Christendom who have argued that when we have the substance, we can dispense with the forms altogether.

The point which no doubt presents the greatest difficulty is the statement that the ordinances of the law were efficacious means of salvation by faith in Christ to the people of the Old Testament. If Christ is "the substance" of the covenant of grace, how could the covenant be dispensed before "the substance was exhibited"? The answer to this difficult question can only be sought in the light of the covenant itself, which stands for a durable structural relationship. Though the temporal mission of Christ is of central and decisive importance in the work of grace, it is not to be thought of as an isolated act, still less as an act which signifies a change in the disposition of God toward sinful men; it is the expression of his eternal purpose of grace which forms the framework of all his dealings with men. The mission of Christ is an event in time, but it is the event that seals the covenant of grace, which is for all times. If we, who look back to it, can participate in it as a present reality, why should not the people of the Old Testament, who looked forward to it, do the same?

■ chapter VIII

OF CHRIST THE MEDIATOR

CF VIII, 1   It pleased God, in his eternal purpose, to choose and ordain the Lord Jesus, his only begotten Son, to be the mediator between God and man, the prophet, priest, and king; the head and saviour of his church, the heir of all things, and judge of the world; unto whom he did, from all eternity, give a people to be his seed, and to be by him in time redeemed, called, justified, sanctified, and glorified.

This chapter deals with the theme which lies at the heart of the Christian gospel, salvation through Christ. In seeking to understand this theme, it is obvious that we have to ask two questions, one concerning Christ the Saviour, and the other concerning the salvation he has wrought. In theology these questions are usually dealt with under two headings, the doctrine of the person of Christ and the doctrine of his work. This arrangement is convenient, and it is employed in this chapter of the Confession; Paragraph 2 is devoted to the person of Christ, and those that follow to his work. But the distinction, though convenient, is artificial; for Christ cannot be separated from the work he does. And the Confession recognizes this when it introduces the theme in the first paragraph, in which it presents a comprehensive summary of the doctrine of Christ as a whole. Here the essential unity of person and work are shown by the fact that the mention of Christ's divine Sonship is followed by a list of his titles, which are all functional in character. Who he is cannot be separated from what he does. Some of the points mentioned in this paragraph have been referred to previously, and the rest are more fully developed in the paragraphs that follow.

"It pleased God, in his eternal purpose, to choose and ordain the Lord Jesus." The fact of Christ is introduced under its eternal aspect, which is the theme of the preceding chapter. Though Christ came to accomplish the work of salvation in time, he was eternally chosen for this work which belongs to the purpose of God from all eternity.

"his only begotten Son." (See on CF II, 3.) If the name Jesus belongs properly to the Son incarnate in our human flesh, its use in connection with his eternal election is strange and perhaps comes under the principle referred to in Paragraph 7.

"to be the mediator between God and man." This term is intended to embrace all the work of Christ; everything he did comes under this heading. The corresponding verb, to mediate, is absent from the New Testament, which uses, instead, the verb, to reconcile. Reconciliation is perhaps the better term of the two to describe the work of Christ and to point to the qualifications involved. Mediation in modern speech suggests the arbitration of a dispute, in which the principal qualification required of the mediator is neutrality; but reconciliation suggests the reunion of two persons or parties who have become estranged, and what is requisite in the reconciler is, not so much neutrality, as rather that he should belong to both and be a friend to both. Christ is the Reconciler between God and man, and as such he is both God and man.

"the prophet, priest, and king." These titles spell out in more detail the mediating or reconciling function of Christ, as can be seen by the manner in which they are introduced in the Shorter Catechism, which says (using "Redeemer" as the comprehensive designation of Christ), "Christ, as our Redeemer, executeth the offices of a prophet, of a priest, and of a king . . ." (SC 23). The doctrine of the "threefold office" of Christ as prophet, priest, and king was developed particularly in the theology of the Reformed Churches. It has been generally recognized as a useful guide to the interpretation of the work of Christ in its full scope, and it has the special value of indicating the relation of his work to the preparation for it in the Old Testament. Prophet, priest, and king were all figures in the life of Israel, but they were more than organs of that life; they were officers of the covenant, which was the foundation of the life of Israel. The prophet was essentially a spokesman for God, one whose mission it was to interpret the acts by which God was leading his people to the fulfillment of his covenant-purpose with them. The priest's vocation was to administer the means which God had provided for the maintenance of the covenant relation by the expiation of sin. The king, though he was a somewhat ambiguous figure, was regarded as the guardian and leader of the covenant people, and despite the failure of the kingship (or perhaps because of it), he came to form the mold of the Messianic hope, in which the old covenant culminated. This hope is realized in Jesus Christ, in whom the offices of prophet, priest, and king are uniquely combined and perfectly fulfilled.

The prophetic office of Christ is defined in the Shorter Catechism as his "revealing to us, by his word and Spirit, the will of God for our salvation" (SC 24); it refers primarily, though not exclusively, to the words he spoke. It has become customary to speak of the words of Jesus as his "teaching," but the term is misleading if it suggests a species of education, even if it be religious and moral education. Jesus was certainly a teacher, and much of his teaching has the form of statements about God and imperatives for human conduct. But it must not be separated from its context in his mission as the Mediator. His words deliver and expound the message of reconciliation. The words with which he opened his public ministry, according to the earliest Gospel, really form the text of all his words: "The time is fulfilled, and the kingdom of God is at hand: repent ye, and believe the gospel." (Mark 1:15.) All the "teaching" of Jesus, the Sermon on the Mount, the parables, the discourses to his disciples, etc., should be regarded as an extended series of sermons on this text, consisting of illustrations of the coming kingdom and expositions of the life of repentance, the life which is turned around and reoriented toward the kingdom when the good news of its coming is received in faith. For this reason Jesus is more aptly described as a prophet than as a teacher.

The priestly office of Christ refers to his atoning work, which is presented in Paragraphs 4 and 5, and to his perpetual intercession, which is mentioned in Paragraph 8.

The title of "king" represents the Biblical terms "Messiah" and "Christ," which both mean "the anointed one," and it points to the part he plays in the fulfillment of God's purpose with his covenant people. The thought is not that of the authority and power which are associated with monarchy—a conception which Jesus himself expressly repudiated (Mark 10:42-45)—but rather that he is the head of a real community which does and can live under his rule. He is the king of a kingdom, which cannot be separated from him. Faith in Christ means more than acknowledging his *claim* or *title* to be king of our lives in some interior or subjective sense; it means becoming citizens of the kingdom, of which he is the king.

"the head and saviour of his church, the heir of all things, and judge of the world; unto whom he did, from all eternity, give a people to be his seed . . ." These titles spell out more fully the meaning of the kingship of Christ. It refers primarily to his church. By its mention of the church in this context the Confession faithfully reflects the teaching of the New Testament on the close and indissoluble union between Christ and his church, which is like that between the bridegroom and the bride. (Eph. 5:22-32.) Christ cannot be rightly understood apart from his church; for it is of the essence of his mediatorial work to establish a community which lives and coheres by it, i.e., a community whose members know themselves to be accepted by God in Christ and who, in the power of that acceptance, also accept one another. (Rom. 15:7.)

Although the kingship of Christ is thus related to the church, that is not to say that the church is identical with the kingdom of God, as Roman Catholics hold. The coming of the kingdom is the final hope of the church. The church consists of the people who acknowledge Christ as king and who are accompanying him on the way to the kingdom; they are the people who receive the gospel of the kingdom (Mark 1:15), who seek the kingdom (Matt. 6:33), who pray for the coming of the kingdom (Matt. 6:10), and to whom the kingdom will be given (Luke 12:32). The church's faith in Christ looks beyond his present relation to it as its head and saviour. It looks forward in hope to his coming again as heir of all things and judge of the world. So, to belong to the church means to belong to the company who are on the move with Christ to the coming of the kingdom, when he will fulfill the purpose of God with his whole creation and effect the final judgment of God upon the world, including the church itself. And because it is thus on the move with Christ toward the fulfillment of the purpose of God, the church is a body which is being continually transformed, as its members are "by him . . . redeemed, called, justified, sanctified, and glorified." This dynamic and "eschatological" element is indigenous to faith in Christ; without it, faith can only wilt and wither.

CF VIII,2   The Son of God, the second person in the Trinity, being very and eternal God, of one substance, and equal with the Father, did, when the fullness of time was come, take upon him man's nature, with all the essential properties and common infirmities thereof; yet without sin: being conceived by the power of the Holy Ghost, in the womb of the Virgin Mary, of her substance. So that two whole, perfect, and distinct natures, the Godhead and the manhood, were inseparably joined together in one person, without conversion, composition, or confusion. Which person is very God and very man, yet one Christ, the only mediator between God and man.

This paragraph deals with Christology or the doctrine of "the person of Christ," and it reproduces the principal features of the orthodox doctrine as it was established, after much controversy and debate, at the Council of Chalcedon in A.D. 451. The doctrine can be summarized in the phrase, "two natures in one person"; it affirms that the Son of God, who is "very [i.e., true] and eternal God," God in person and God in nature, also took upon him the nature of man, deriving it from the substance of humanity through the Virgin Mary, of whom he was born, and joining it to his divine nature within the unity of his person. The church believed that the truth about Christ had to be stated in this way if it was to be preserved from error and corruption. With this formula the church gave what it believed to be the definitive answer to the question posed by the figure of Jesus Christ as he is presented in the pages of the New Testament.

To understand the answer given in the Christological formula it is best to begin with the question posed by the figure of the Gospel records, more especially as it has often been contended that the Christological formula is a fabrication of hair-splitting intellectuals and bears no relation to the figure portrayed in the pages of the Gospels. Who is Jesus Christ? Does the question, as it is posed by the records, require the answer given in the orthodox doctrine?

Some have held that it is sufficient to regard Jesus Christ as a man, a great man, indeed, who has made a tremendous impress on human history, but not essentially different from other great men who have also left their mark. The ordinary secular historian usually represents Christ in this way, and indeed, he has no choice; for he has no categories other than human in which to account for figures of history. Moreover, these categories do, in fact, enable him to present a plausible account of Jesus Christ; for even on the basis of such evidence as the historian can recognize, it appears to be incontestable that he really existed and that he has exerted an influence comparable to that of the greatest men who have marched across the stage of history. The figure of Jesus has sometimes been placed alongside Socrates and Confucius and others in a portrait gallery of the world's great men, and if great men are those who have exercised a decisive influence on history, it may be said that no such gallery would be complete without him. The Christian faith has no reason to quarrel with this evaluation of the historical significance of Jesus Christ as a human figure; for it is a vital element in the Christian doctrine of Christ that he was true man, and if he was true man, then he is open to comparison with other men and to classification in the common categories of humanity.

The question is whether he is adequately accounted for in this way; and the answer is that he is not, not even at the historical level. For the records of his life show that his appearance on the stage of history had the effect of raising the question of his person in such a way that it could not be answered in the ordinary categories of historical interpretation. This is, in fact, a main theme of the Gospel narratives. His appearance at the beginning of his public ministry had the immediate effect of raising the questions, Who is this that teaches with authority? (Mark 1:27); Who is this that forgives sins? (Mark 2:7); Who then is this, that even wind and sea obey him? (Mark 4:41). He himself confronted his disciples with the question, first asking them, "Whom do men say that I am?" and then, "But whom say ye that I am?" (Mark 8:27-29.) The question acted as a catalyst to precipitate the division between those who were for and those who were against him (see John 6:66-71); and from this point the life of Jesus enters an increasingly critical phase until it culminates in his trial by the Jewish and Roman authorities, in which the decisive question is, Who is he? (See Mark 14:61.) The Gospels clearly mean to indicate that this was no accidental effect but was the intention of his appearance, in the sense that men could have no real encounter with Jesus Christ unless they felt themselves confronted with this question in a decisive way.

It is further clear that the question was not whether Jesus was to be given a place of pre-eminence and clothed with the highest superlatives as the best, the purest, the noblest of men, though this was a plausible approach and one which evidently appealed to many of his contemporaries; for the answers they are reported to have given to the question of his identity—John the Baptist, Elijah, one of the prophets (Mark 8:27-28)—are all attempts to place him among the great and outstanding figures in the nation's history. And they were right in that; Jesus certainly belongs in this group. But what the episode of Caesarea Philippi brings out, and what the subsequent history up to the trial makes conclusively clear, is that the real issue was not whether the question is to be answered in positives or superlatives but whether it can be answered in human categories at all. The proceedings at the trial make it unmistakably plain that the charge against Jesus was not that of claiming some human eminence for himself; it was that of asserting, explicitly or implicitly, that he was God. And it was more than a matter of words—in fact, the Gospels record a somewhat puzzling reticence or reserve on the part of Jesus (e.g., Mark 8:30); his actions carried the implication that the subject of them was God, in such a way that if it were not so, his whole life would be one grand imposture.

But how could Jesus Christ be both God and man, as Christian faith confesses him to be? The doctrinal statement given in the Confession is best understood if we consider first why the claim of Christ was rejected by the authorities at his trial. It was rejected by both the Jewish and the Roman authorities, and for much the same reasons. To the Jews the distance between the Creator and the creatures was so great that the idea of an equation between the Creator and any creature was nothing short of blasphemous. (John 5:18; Mark 14:64.) And Pilate's whole attitude, his inability to take Christ seriously and his disposition to dismiss him as a harmless crank, points to a similar presupposition in his mind; it was preposterous that the man before him should really be what he claimed or was alleged to be.

The behavior of both Pilate and the Jews reflects the general sense of mankind that between the divine and the human there is a great gulf fixed and that all crossing from one side to the other is out of the question. Does the confession of Christian faith that Jesus Christ is both God and man involve the denial of this presupposition? Does Christian faith, in other words, contend that the distance between the human and the divine is not so great as it has been supposed to be? The question is asked because it would seem to open the way to a relatively easy solution of the Christological problem—one which, in fact, has been often taken, and which is probably taken, consciously or unconsciously, by many today. If the difference between human and divine be reduced to a difference of degree, it might then be thought possible, by ascending the scale of humanity to its highest peak of moral and spiritual elevation, to reach a point where it merges in divinity; divinity, so to speak, would be equivalent to humanity raised to the nth degree.

The potential divinization of humanity may be discerned as a motif in the popular piety of Roman Catholicism, in the veneration of the saints, and especially in the adoration of the Virgin Mary, who, having begun life as a real woman of human clay and human frailty, has, as the result of successive dogmatic operations, been transformed into a semi-divine being, the object of something akin to divine honors, and, who, it is now thought, is on her way to being proclaimed co-redemptrix, partner with her Son in the redemption of the world. It may also be seen, at the opposite end of the scale, in some types of Unitarianism, where there is a disposition to concede the divinity of Christ provided it be taken in a sense which precludes any essential difference between his divinity and the divinity (actual or potential) of all men.

The orthodox doctrine of the church has always rejected this approach. In the words of the Confession, which echo those of the definition of Chalcedon, it has stressed that "two whole, perfect, and distinct natures, the Godhead and the manhood, were inseparably joined together in one person, *without conversion, composition, or confusion.*" The emphasis is on the final phrase, which is intended to rule out any thought of a merger between the natures as such. Godhead and manhood were not joined together in such a way that one was converted into the other, humanity into divinity or divinity into humanity; nor were they compounded in such a way as to produce a dual nature, partly human and partly divine; nor were they fused together so as to produce a third kind of nature, neither human nor divine, but something different. The orthodox doctrine, that is to say, accepts the presupposition on which the Jewish and the Roman authorities denied the divinity of Christ, namely, that humanity and divinity are so distinct and discontinuous that there can be no merging of one with the other. And this is no arbitrary presupposition, but was endorsed by Christ himself in his reply to Peter's confession at Caesarea Philippi, "Blessed art thou, Simon Bar-jona: for flesh and blood hath not revealed it unto thee" (Matt. 16:17); divinity cannot be deduced or inferred from any qualities, however superlative, that may be observed in the humanity; it is a confession of faith, not a judgment of value.

If the two natures are not joined together by conversion or composition or confusion, how then are they joined? The answer is that they are "inseparably joined together in one person"; i.e., the uniting factor is in the *person* of Christ, not in the natures themselves. The union of the natures is a personal, not a natural union.

It is clear that everything hinges on the distinction in meaning between "nature" and "person." But this distinction is not easy to express. The terms do not bear the same meanings in Christological doctrine as they do in modern English, or even in the New Testament, where both of them occur. (Compare Heb. 1:3; II Peter 1:4.) It may be sufficient to say that the distinction between them is broadly that "nature" gives the answer to the question What? and "person" gives the answer to the question Who? The ancient Greeks, who devised this terminology, observed that there are two elements, or two sides, to being a human being. On the one hand, a human being can be defined in terms of a group of properties and attributes, so that anyone who possesses these can be said to be a human being according to definition. If a human being is defined, for example, as a rational animal, body and mind would be the essential attributes of a human being, and anyone possessing them would satisfy the definition; if I have a body and a mind, I am a human being. But the very language we use itself points to the other element involved; for body and mind are things which I *have*, they belong to me, but they are not identical with me. I would not say I *am* a body and a mind. Even though I could not be myself without my body and my mind, the real I, the real self, is not identical with any of my parts, faculties, or functions, nor with the sum of all of them together. It is "something which underlies" them— this is the literal meaning of the Greek word (*hypostasis*) which is translated "person"; it points to what I mean when I say "I"; it is the center of my being and the subject of all my experiences. The Christological doctrine affirms that Christ was "one person," i.e., one personal self or subject.

How was it possible for Christ to be one person in this sense and at the same time to unite in his one person two natures? This is the most difficult question, and one with which the mind of the church has never ceased to wrestle. There are some who contend that the purpose of the Christological formula is not to *explain*, but only to *safeguard*, the mystery which lies at the heart of the Christian faith: namely, that he who is true God became also true man, lived a true human life, and underwent a true human experience. Devout acknowledgment of the mystery, however, is not necessarily incompatible with attempts to probe it. Such attempts have been made from the beginning, and some of the more important of them may be briefly indicated here.

(1) One of the oldest of them is referred to in Paragraph 7:

CF VIII,7   Christ, in the work of mediation, acteth according to both natures; by each nature doing that which is proper to itself; yet by reason of the unity of the person, that which is proper to one nature is sometimes, in Scripture, attributed to the person denominated by the other nature.

This paragraph summarizes the idea of alternation or departmentalization, propounded in a famous papal document known as *Leo's Tome*, which was submitted to the Council of Chalcedon and had much influence with its members. According to this idea, Christ, though uniting in his person two natures, uses them, as it were, separately, or alternately, switching from one to the other as occasion requires. Thus everything in Christ which manifests weakness—his hunger, his thirst, his suffering—are held to belong to his human nature, while his miracles and other acts of power belong to the divine.

The idea of two natures related in this way seems somewhat mechanical, though perhaps not necessarily so, and it seems to come close to what is now called a dual personality. The most serious question would be whether a being who has at his command a human nature and a divine, and who can move from one to the other, presumably at will, could be called a true man.

(2) Considerable vogue was enjoyed in the nineteenth century by the kenotic theory. The name is derived from the Greek word which is translated, "[he] emptied himself" (Phil. 2:7, rsv), and which was interpreted by some to mean that in taking "the form of a servant" Christ relinquished "the form of God," or, in other words, that in becoming man, he stripped himself of his divinity and all its attributes—to resume them at his exaltation. The difficulty of the theory is that it would make Christ incarnate a "mere man" (SC 82); even if he had formerly been God, he could not be said to unite Godhead and manhood in one person, and he would lack the essential qualification for acting as the mediator between God and man. Moreover, it is extremely difficult to conceive how one who was God could cease to be God.

(3) One of the earliest attempts to solve the problem was to deny that Christ was essentially or eternally God and to regard him, instead, as a uniquely good man who was (at his baptism) adopted into union with God. The presupposition of the adoptionist theory, as it is called, is that there is some quality about the humanity of Christ that lends it to union with divinity. Repeated attempts have been made to build a bridge between the humanity and the divinity in this way, and one may be seen in the mystical type of approach which is widely favored in modern Christology. Employing the mystical principle that the way to union with God is by self-negation, or self-emptying, this type of Christology presents the humanity of Christ as some sort of vac-

uum which was fitted to be filled with the divine.[1] But if the presence of God in Christ is contingent on some quality in his humanity, this reduces the difference between Christ and others to one of degree only; Christ is then only the man in whom the condition to which all mystics have aspired is perfectly realized. The theory is also open to the more serious objection, from the standpoint of traditional orthodoxy, that it presupposes a certain continuity, even if only of a negative character, between humanity and divinity, which is incompatible with the principle of the inconfusability of the two natures which was affirmed at Chalcedon and is endorsed in the Confession.

(4) It is possible that the best approach to the problem is to think of the humanity as the *form* of the divinity, and perhaps Philippians 2:5-11, which was used as the basis of the kenotic theory, intends us to think of it in this way; namely, that Christ, being in the form of God, took the form of a servant, not in order to cease to be God, but in order to be God in human form. Perhaps also the classical doctrine, as it is stated in the Confession, points in this direction; for when it says that "The Son of

---

[1] A famous example of the mystical type of approach to Christology was that of Schleiermacher, who taught that the place normally occupied in human nature by self-consciousness was in Christ wholly occupied by God-consciousness; the God-consciousness, which is only weakly present in most men, was of such a superlative degree of strength in Christ as to constitute "a veritable existence of God in Him." (Friedrich Schleiermacher, *The Christian Faith*, English Translation, p. 385. Edinburgh: T. & T. Clark, 1928.) D. M. Baillie uses the Christian experience of grace as his clue. Grace is the experience in which a man claims no credit to himself for any good he has done, but ascribes it all to God. The man Jesus Christ is the supreme example of this: "In the New Testament we see the man in whom God was incarnate surpassing all other men in refusing to claim anything for Himself independently and ascribing all the goodness to God." (D. M. Baillie, *God Was in Christ*, p. 117. New York: Charles Scribner's Sons, 1948.) And Paul Tillich says it is because Jesus sacrificed himself and all his finite concerns that he became the bearer of the final revelation of God; by his complete self-negation he became completely "transparent" to the divine mystery. (*Systematic Theology*, Vol. I, pp. 132-137. Chicago: University of Chicago Press, 1951.)

God, the second person in the Trinity, being very and eternal God . . . did . . . take upon him man's nature," it makes it clear that there is a disparity between the two natures. The divine nature is integral to the person of the Son of God, while the human nature is *taken,* and it was further explained by some of the Fathers that the human nature was to be understood as impersonal in itself and as acquiring personality only when it was taken into the person of the Son of God. It would seem, therefore, that when they spoke of Christ as uniting two natures in one person, they meant to say that while he was a divine person and the subject of a divine nature and experience, he chose to be this in the form of a human nature and experience. Being God, he chose to become man, and so to be *God as man,* living his life under the conditions of human life.

If it be said that this conception reduces the humanity of Christ to the level of a dramatic role which he chose to play, it is surely sufficient, in reply, to point to the realism with which he played it, right to the bitter end: "And being found in fashion as a man, he humbled himself, and became obedient unto death, even the death of the cross." (Phil. 2:8.) And if it be said that the conception of the humanity as the form of the divinity conflicts with the principle of the distinctness and inconfusability of the two natures, on which the church has always laid so great emphasis, it may be replied that the principle was primarily directed against any thought of a continuity between the human and the divine which would make possible an ascent from humanity to divinity or a divinization of humanity; it cannot be used to deny the freedom of God in his grace to enter into the condition and experience of man, his creature.[2]

---

[2] The mystery of the person of Christ is, of course, unique, and it cannot be explained in the light of anything to be found in the realm of human experience. But since even a partial understanding of the mystery is impossible except in the light of some analogy derived from human experience, it may be pointed out that human experience abounds in analogies to the interpretation which is suggested above, whereby Christ assumed humanity as the form of his divinity and so became God as man. The phrase, "putting

CF VIII,3   The Lord Jesus in his human nature thus united to the divine, was sanctified and anointed with the Holy Spirit above measure; having in him all the treasures of wisdom and knowledge, in whom it pleased the Father that all fullness should dwell: to the end that being holy, harmless, undefiled, and full of grace and truth, he might be thoroughly furnished to execute the office of a mediator and surety. Which office he took not unto himself, but was thereunto called by his Father; who put all power and judgment into his hand, and gave him commandment to execute the same.

The mediator between God and man must be able to deal with man on behalf of God and with God on behalf of man. This paragraph states his qualifications to act for God. These qualifications, which pertain to him "in his human nature thus united to the divine" (and are not, therefore, to be thought of as the source or ground of his divinity), are principally superlative en-

---

ourselves in someone else's shoes," expresses an identification of ourselves with others, which is often asked of us in imagination, and which is an indispensable requirement in certain professions, such as teaching; a good teacher must be able to put himself in the place of the pupil and view the subject of instruction from the standpoint of the pupil. In doing this he does not cease to be a teacher—for to do so would be to defeat the educational process—but, without ceasing to be a teacher or renouncing the knowledge and experience of a teacher, he encloses it in the knowledge and experience of the pupil. An even better example would be the French "worker-priests." These priests, concerned about the failure of the church to "get across" to the workers, decided that they would go across to the workers and become workers themselves. So they took jobs in factories and went to live in workers' quarters and subsist on workers' wages. They assumed the conditions under which they could enter fully into the life and experience of the workers. They did not cease to be priests; by the performance of the minimal daily duties of priests they maintained their status and experience as priests. But by becoming workers, they enclosed their priestly experience in the form of workers' experience and so became priests in the form of workers.

dowment with the Holy Spirit and divine appointment. The distinctive feature of the bestowal of the Holy Spirit on Jesus ("above measure"; compare John 3:34) is that the gift is permanent (John 1:32-33) and that he himself dispenses it to others (Mark 1:8-10). The phrases which follow spell out the meaning of this gift; they say, in effect, that by his endowment with the Holy Spirit Jesus is uniquely qualified to interpret the mind and will and heart of God, and so to say to men, "I am the way, the truth, and the life." (John 14:6.) The necessity of divine appointment for anyone who is to act for God with full authority is self-evident. This is the meaning of the term Christ, or Messiah, which designates the one divinely anointed to fulfill God's purpose with his people. It is curious that the Confession here uses the name of Christ only in Paragraphs 2 and 6-8, while in Paragraphs 1 and 3-5 it speaks of the Lord Jesus.

CF VIII,4   This office the Lord Jesus did most willingly undertake, which, that he might discharge, he was made under the law, and did perfectly fulfill it; endured most grievous torments immediately in his soul, and most painful sufferings in his body; was crucified and died; was buried, and remained under the power of death, yet saw no corruption. On the third day he arose from the dead, with the same body in which he suffered; with which also he ascended into heaven, and there sitteth at the right hand of his Father, making intercession; and shall return to judge men and angels, at the end of the world.

This paragraph deals with the other side of the mediatorial task and states what was involved in Christ's acting for man. First is his free, personal acceptance of the task, for it is plain that without this, reconciliation, or the restoration of right personal relations between God and man, could not be effected. The next thing is his assumption of man's condition and situation. This means more than his assumption of man's nature, which is dealt with in Paragraph 2; it means his identification of himself with man and his putting himself in the place where man actually stands before God. He became subject to the law, like every other man, and he exposed himself to the judgment of the law and endured the pain which it entails, both inward and outward, though, for himself, his obedience to the law was perfect. And having set foot on this road he traveled it right to the end; having lived the life of man, he also died his death. But though he died the death of man, his death was not the end but the beginning of the new life; it was the climactic point at which his acting in behalf of man was intersected by his acting in behalf of God. The cross of Christ, by its very shape, points to the miracle whereby his death was crossed or canceled by the Resurrection, and this not through any quality of his manhood which enabled him to cheat the mechanism of death, but by the power of God who was in him.

"with the same body in which he suffered; with which also he ascended into heaven . . ." The emphasis on the identity of the body of Christ crucified and risen is not so much for its own sake as because it is the body of his identification with us. His resurrection is the pledge of ours (I Cor. 15); "because I live, ye shall live also" (John 14:19). It is as our representative that he was raised and exalted and is also appointed the final judge of all men. (See Acts 17:31.) In him the ultimate destiny of our reconciled and renewed humanity is eternally assured.

CF VIII,5   The Lord Jesus, by his perfect obedience and sacrifice of himself, which he through the eternal Spirit once offered up unto God, hath fully satisfied the justice of his Father; and purchased not only reconciliation, but an everlasting inheritance in the kingdom of heaven, for all those whom the Father hath given unto him.

The heart of the mediatorial work of Christ, which he executes as priest (see SC 25), is the work of reconciliation, or atonement. To the question how Christ accomplished this work many answers have been given; and though there is no one answer which can claim the exclusive endorsement of the New Testament, there are some which are incompatible with the witness of the New Testament.

"by his perfect obedience and sacrifice of himself." The double phrase points to the important truth, which has often been overlooked, that the atoning work should not be associated exclusively with his death, but belongs to his life as well. Both his life and his death are included in his obedience (they used to be called his active and his passive obedience), and they should be looked at together. If we wish to know the meaning of the death of Christ, we must look for it in his life, of which his death is the consummation.

"through the eternal Spirit." This phrase is used in Hebrews 9:14, in a passage which contrasts the sacrifice of Christ with the animal sacrifices of the old dispensation; while the latter could effect only a temporary and ceremonial or external purification, the sacrifice which Christ "once offered" (i.e., once for all) is able to purify the conscience and secure an eternal redemption, since he offered himself freely and willingly (Par. 4), through the Spirit of God, by whom all his actions were directed (Par. 3).

"hath fully satisfied the justice of his Father." The interpretation of the atoning work of Christ which is presented here is one which enjoyed a great vogue in the church, both Roman Catholic and Protestant, but which is unbiblical. It combines a genuinely Biblical conception (sacrifice) with another (satisfaction) which is not Biblical. The theory that Christ by his obedience and sacrifice satisfied the justice of God and so made it possible for God to grant forgiveness to sinful men was first propounded in the early Middle Ages by Anselm (1033-1109), who probably spun it out of the concept of satisfaction employed in the Roman sacrament of penance. In no passage in the New Testament where the death of Christ is represented as a sacrifice is it suggested that it produced an effect on God, either in the "satisfaction" of his "justice" or in the alteration of his disposition toward men. On the contrary, whenever mention is made of the effect of Christ's sacrifice, it is of the effect on those on whose behalf the sacrifice is offered. (See Heb. 9:9, 14; 10:10, 14; 13:12.) The theory of Anselm, reflected in the Confession, that the sacrifice of Christ fulfilled a legal requirement on the part of God, is incompatible with the central evangelical message of the New Testament, that forgiveness is the free gift of God, that it flows spontaneously from his love (John 3:16), and that it does not first have to be procured from him by the fulfillment of some condition on the part of Christ.

"and purchased not only reconciliation." Both "purchase" and "reconciliation" are terms used in the New Testament in connection with the atoning work of Christ, but nowhere in the New Testament are they combined in this way. Reconciliation is not purchased from God by the work of Christ; it is the work of God in Christ: "All this is from God, who through Christ reconciled us to himself . . . God was in Christ reconciling the world to himself." (II Cor. 5:18-19, RSV.) The term "purchase" belongs to a different context, namely, the idea of "redemption." Redemption, which was a familiar practice in the ancient world in connection with the liberation of slaves, the ransoming of captives, and the redemption of pledged goods, is frequently employed in the New Testament as a figure for the atoning work of Christ, and it has a basis in his own saying about giving his life "a ransom for many." (Mark 10:45.) But what is "purchased" (Acts 20:28), or "bought" (I Cor. 6:20; 7:23), or "redeemed" (I Peter 1:18) is always sinful men and women, and it is *for* God that they are purchased, never from him. If the figure is taken literally and the idea of purchase is pressed, consistency would require us to infer that the payment was made to the powers of evil which held men in bondage; the theory was long current in the early church that the ransom was paid to the devil, on the basis of Hebrews 2:14-15. But this kind of language is obviously figurative in this context; it points to the costliness of the atoning work of Christ, but it should not be pressed in a literal sense.

"an everlasting inheritance." Reconciliation to God through Christ is not only for now but for ever. It opens up a new future in eternal fellowship with God and makes the man who is reconciled a man of inextinguishable hope. (Rom. 5:1-5.)

CF VIII,6   Although the work of redemption was not actually wrought by Christ till after his incarnation, yet the virtue, efficacy, and benefits thereof were communicated unto the elect, in all ages successively from the beginning of the world, in and by those promises, types, and sacrifices wherein he was revealed, and signified to be the seed of the woman, which should bruise the serpent's head, and the lamb slain from the beginning of the world, being yesterday and today the same and for ever.

This paragraph returns to the point already touched on in CF VII, 5, concerning the availability of the benefits of the work of Christ to those who lived in the period which is called "B.C." (before Christ). If the work of Christ was wrought at a specific date in history ("under Pontius Pilate," as the Apostles' Creed says), how could it be enjoyed by those who lived before that date? Ordinarily historical events cannot be anticipated. The discovery of penicillin in World War II, for instance, could be of no help to the wounded in World War I. Yet the very nature of faith in Christ forbids the thought that all who lived before his advent, together with those beyond reach of the gospel or too young to grasp it (XII, 3), should be excommunicate. The Confession here restates the position taken in CF VII, 5, where the mission of Christ is presented in the context of the covenant of grace; although the covenant of grace involves the coming of Christ in history, his presence is not limited to the time of his historical presence but was mediated in advance through the promises and ordinances of the old dispensation to those who lived before that time, as it is mediated to us, who live after it, by the word and sacraments.

The truth of the pre-incarnational efficacy of the work of Christ, important as it is to faith, cannot, however, be based on the passages adduced to support it. The passage in Genesis 3:15, which speaks of enmity between the serpent and the woman and their respective seeds, was long regarded as the "protevangelium" or first intimation of the gospel of the victory of Christ, but in all probability it refers to the loss of the harmony between man and the animal creation which is a consequence of the fall. Revelation 13:8 is more correctly translated in the Revised Standard Version: "every one whose name has not been written before the foundation of the world in the book of life of the Lamb that was slain." Nevertheless there is a sense in which it may be truly said that the cross is engraved upon the heart of God from all eternity. Christ is "the substance" of the covenant of grace (CF VII, 6) who fulfills the eternal purpose of God with man, and as such he is the same yesterday and today and for ever.

CF VIII,8   To all those for whom Christ hath purchased redemption, he doth certainly and effectually apply and communicate the same; making intercession for them, and revealing unto them, in and by the word, the mysteries of salvation; effectually persuading them by his Spirit to believe and obey; and governing their hearts by his word and Spirit; overcoming all their enemies by his almighty power and wisdom, in such manner and ways as are most consonant to his wonderful and unsearchable dispensation.

Two important truths are indicated in this paragraph. (1) As the chapter begins by affirming the authenticity of the work of Christ as the realization of the eternal purpose of God (Par. 1), it concludes by pointing to the efficacy of his work among men. As Christ really comes from God, so he really reaches men and communicates to them the divine gift he bears. The purpose of God to reconcile, which is expressed in Christ (II Cor. 5:19), is realized in the existence of a reconciled people, people who actually live by the work of Christ. The work of Christ is efficacious in the lives of men. This must not, of course, be taken pragmatically as a *proof* of the faith that God was in Christ; nevertheless it is an integral element of that faith. The Apostles' Creed bids us profess our faith, not only in God and in Christ and in the Holy Spirit, but also in the holy catholic church, the communion of saints, the forgiveness of sins, the resurrection of the body, and the life everlasting; that is, a society of people who are bound together by the love of Christ, who accept his forgiveness as the ground on which they stand by faith, and who look to a future which is shaped and determined by hope in him. (2) The efficacy of the work of Christ is not limited to those who were contemporaneous with the historical performance of it, but, as it was extended to those who lived before that time (B.C.), it is also extended to those who come after (A.D.). This is the meaning of the references to the Spirit, who comes after the departure of the incarnate Christ (John 16:7) and whose mission it is to communicate Christ's work to men (John 16:14-15). The Spirit is the theme of the next chapter. It should also be noted that the terms in which the continuing work of Christ is described here reflect the threefold office as prophet ("revealing" and "persuading"), priest ("making intercession"), and king ("governing" and "overcoming"), with the emphasis placed more on the internal aspects of it.

■ note on chapters IX and X

The two chapters which follow did not belong to the Confession of Faith in its original form but were added during the present century in order to give clearer and fuller expression to certain articles of faith which, it was felt, had not been adequately treated. The chapters were prepared by a committee appointed by the General Assembly of the Presbyterian Church in the USA and were adopted by the Assembly at its meeting in 1903, with the preamble: "Whereas, it is desirable to express more fully the doctrine of the Church concerning the Holy Spirit, Missions, and the Love of God for all men, the following chapters are added to the Confession of Faith." The chapters were placed at the end of the Confession and given the numbers XXXIV and XXXV, the latter having the title, "Of the Love of God and Missions."[1] They were subsequently adopted by the General Assembly of the Presbyterian Church in the US in 1942 and incorporated in the Confession as Chapters IX and X; Chapter X was given a new title, "Of the Gospel."

---

[1] For a full account see Lefferts A. Loetscher, *The Broadening Church* (Philadelphia: University of Pennsylvania Press, 1954), Chapter 10, "Revision Accomplished," pp. 83-89.

■ chapter IX[1]

OF THE HOLY SPIRIT

The absence of a chapter on the Holy Spirit from the original Confession is not easy to account for. It cannot be ascribed to ignorance of the work of the Spirit; for that is referred to in many places. Indeed, the claim has been made, with some truth, that this added chapter contains no substantial addition to the teaching on the Spirit which is scattered throughout the Confession, but merely gathers it together and presents it in systematic form. While that may be true, the fact that the original authors of the Confession did not see fit to concentrate their teaching on the Spirit in one chapter may be held to indicate a certain insensitivity to the real import and significance of the theme which was characteristic of the theological thinking of their period. If it be true that the Holy Spirit points to the creativity, the freedom, and the inwardness of the work of God, it could be said that the Westminster Confession of Faith reflects a type of theology which tends to stabilize the relations between God and man within the framework of a rigid system, in which the freedom of God himself is circumscribed (see the doctrine of predestination), and which makes it difficult to distinguish the inwardness of faith from intellectual acceptance of a doctrinal system. A confession of faith which contains a chapter on the Holy Spirit is thereby reminded of the limited scope and function of all doctrinal formulations, which can point toward the gospel but can never contain it.

---

[1] Chapter XXXIV in the Confession of Faith of the United Presbyterian Church in the USA.

CF IX,1   The Holy Spirit, the third person in the Trinity, proceeding from the Father and the Son, of the same substance and equal in power and glory, is, together with the Father and the Son, to be believed in, loved, obeyed, and worshipped throughout all ages.

See on CF II, 3.

CF IX,2   He is the Lord and Giver of life, everywhere present, and is the source of all good thoughts, pure desires, and holy counsels in men. By him the prophets were moved to speak the word of God, and all the writers of the Holy Scriptures inspired to record infallibly the mind and will of God. The dispensation of the gospel is especially committed to him. He prepares the way for it, accompanies it with his persuasive power, and urges its message upon the reason and conscience of men, so that they who reject its merciful offer are not only without excuse, but are also guilty of resisting the Holy Spirit.

The English word "spirit," like its equivalents in Hebrew and Greek, is connected with breath, which marks the presence of life. The Spirit of God is the source of all life, and more particularly of the life of man, which is more than mere animation; it is a life which a-*spires* toward its origin. The manifestation of the Spirit in the orientation of man toward God is the counterpart of his work in the orientation of God toward man, in the in-*spir*ation of those who were called to bear witness to the word by which he calls man into fellowship with himself. And the fulfillment of the word in the gospel of Christ does not render the work of the Spirit superfluous, but rather marks the fulfillment of the work of the Spirit in both its aspects; for now the Spirit, "which is from God" and reveals "the depths of God" (I Cor. 2:10-12, RSV), coincides with the answering echo in man and "beareth witness with our spirit, that we are the children of God" (Rom. 8:16).

CF IX,3   The Holy Spirit, whom the Father is ever willing

to give to all who ask him, is the only efficient agent in the application of redemption. He regenerates men by his grace, convicts them of sin, moves them to repentance, and persuades and enables them to embrace Jesus Christ by faith. He unites all believers to Christ, dwells in them as their Comforter and Sanctifier, gives to them the spirit of Adoption and Prayer, and performs all those gracious offices by which they are sanctified and sealed unto the day of redemption.

This paragraph deals with the inward aspect of the work of the Spirit in connection with "the dispensation of the gospel," which is described as his special commission in Paragraph 2. This evangelical work consists in the creation of a new life in man ("regenerates"), a life which is severed from sin and self and united by faith to Jesus Christ, who by his indwelling Spirit transforms them and sets them in motion toward the hope of a new and eternal future.

CF IX,4   By the indwelling of the Holy Spirit all believers being vitally united to Christ, who is the Head, are thus united one to another in the church, which is his body. He calls and anoints ministers for their holy office, qualifies all other officers in the church for their special work, and imparts various gifts and graces to its members. He gives efficacy to the word and to the ordinances of the gospel. By him the church will be preserved, increased, purified, and at last made perfectly holy in the presence of God.

The indwelling of the Holy Spirit is not a private and individual affair but the source of true community; for the Holy Spirit is a gift which men have only by sharing in it; "the communion of the Holy Spirit," which probably means common participation in the Holy Spirit, unites them to Christ and to one another and so forms them into the body of Christ. Then within the unity of the body of Christ, which is formed by common participation in the gift of the Holy Spirit, special gifts and endowments are given to individual members for the service of the body as a whole. The officers who have received such gifts are not to be thought of as alone possessors of the Holy Spirit—for the presence and activity of the Spirit is the life of the whole body—but they are endowed for the fulfillment of special vocations within the body. Similarly, when it is stated that the efficacy of the function they perform, in the ministry of the Word and the sacraments, depends on the Holy Spirit, the reference is not solely to the special endowments bestowed on them; unless the Spirit opens the minds and hearts of the hearers, as well as the mouth of the preacher, there can be no real communication of the gospel. Not only the life of the church but its continuing growth, its renewal, and the great hope by which it is sustained are ascribed to the presence and power of the Holy Spirit.

▪ chapter X[1]

OF THE GOSPEL

CF X, 1   God in infinite and perfect love, having provided in the covenant of grace, through the mediation and sacrifice of the Lord Jesus Christ, a way of life and salvation, sufficient for and adapted to the whole lost race of man, doth freely offer this salvation to all men in the gospel.

This chapter, as was said in the note preceding Chapter IX, was added to the Confession in response to a widely felt desire for a clearer statement of the universality of the love of God and of the obligation resting upon the church to carry the message of this love into all the world. When the chapter was first adopted by the General Assembly of the Presbyterian Church in the USA, it was accompanied by a Declaratory Statement concerning its relation to Chapter III, in which it was said that "the doctrine of God's eternal decree is held in harmony with the doctrine of his love to all mankind." It may, however, be doubted whether it is logically or theologically possible to harmonize the "some men" of CF III, 3 with the "all men" of X, 1; and it may be suspected that the effect, if not the intention, of Chapter X is to modify or correct the doctrine stated in Chapter III, in the direction indicated in the present commentary.

The first paragraph should be read as a footnote to CF VII,

---

[1] Chapter XXXV in the Confession of Faith of the United Presbyterian Church in the USA, where it is entitled, "Of the Gospel of the Love of God and Missions."

3; it states that, as the actual terms of the gospel offer indicate, the salvation provided in the covenant of grace is in God's eternal purpose intended for all men.

CF X,2   In the gospel God declares his love for the world and his desire that all men should be saved; reveals fully and clearly the only way of salvation; promises eternal life to all who truly repent and believe in Christ; invites and commands all to embrace the offered mercy; and by his Spirit accompanying the word pleads with men to accept his gracious invitation.

The universality of the offer of salvation is shown by the actual terms of the gospel, which contain nothing to suggest any limitation or restriction of it on the part of God.

CF X,3   It is the duty and privilege of everyone who hears the gospel immediately to accept its merciful provisions; and they who continue in impenitence and unbelief incur aggravated guilt and perish by their own fault.

This stress on the responsibility of the hearer of the gospel to decide between acceptance and rejection marks the chief difference between this chapter and Chapter III. The authors of Chapter III, while formally affirming that the sovereignty of the divine will does not violate the will of the creatures, tended to regard any exercise of the latter in relation to the offer of salvation as savoring of Arminianism; it seemed to them that the grace of God would be impugned unless men were "altogether passive therein." (CF XII, 2.) But the gospel of the grace of God does not eliminate responsible decision; on the contrary, it calls men to make the most decisive decision of their lives, and in making it they need have no fear that they are taking part in a farce.

CF X,4   Since there is no other way of salvation than that revealed in the gospel, and since in the divinely established and ordinary method of grace faith cometh by

hearing the word of God, Christ hath commissioned
his church to go into all the world and to make disciples of all nations. All believers are, therefore, under obligation to sustain the ordinances of the Christian religion where they are already established, and to
contribute by their prayers, gifts, and personal efforts
to the extension of the kingdom of Christ throughout
the whole earth.

Belief in the universality of the love of God imposes a corresponding responsibility on the believer; he who believes that
the saving love of God extends to all men must see to it that the
message of that love is heard by all men. It is an historical fact
that when it was thought that God's saving purpose was restricted
to the elect, the church as a whole was remiss in its obedience to
the great commission (Matt. 28:19-20). As the church came to understand that God's purpose of salvation extends to all men, so it
came to recognize its own responsibility for the extension of the
gospel to the ends of the earth. Since the preaching of the gospel
is "the divinely established and ordinary method" of salvation,
the obligation to spread it abroad is inescapable. But this obligation is one that God lays upon us, not one that we lay upon him;
we may not draw the inference that those who have not come
within the sound of the gospel are thereby excluded from salvation.

■ chapter XI[1]

OF FREE WILL

CF XI, 1 God hath endued the will of man with that natural liberty, that it is neither forced, nor by any absolute necessity of nature determined to good or evil.

The freedom of the will is one of the most difficult and baffling problems with which the human mind has wrestled. Some philosophers have argued for the freedom of the will, others have denied it; and both positions have been defended with exceedingly powerful arguments. But, while the debate continues, it has come to be widely recognized that the question is too complex to be answered by a simple Yes or No. To cite the most obvious complication, it is one question whether we are free to *choose* what we do, and it is another question whether we are free to *do* what we choose, and the answers to the two questions may not be the same.

The question is raised in the context of the Christian faith by the nature of the gospel, which calls man to responsible decision. The relation between them is indicated by the introduction of the theme at this point in the Confession. The question is not raised in an abstract or speculative way, nor is it answered with a simple affirmative or a simple negative. The Confession asks what account is to be given of man's freedom in the light of God's dealings with him, and it unfolds the answer in what may be called a theological history of freedom.

---

[1] Chapter IX in the Confession of Faith of the United Presbyterian Church in the USA.

The Confession begins by affirming the formal freedom of the will. It here affirms the position of common sense, which is, as Luther once put it, that the will is really a will and not a "nill." It denies the position of philosophical determinism, which is that the choices we make are determined by some superior necessity and that the freedom we feel in making them is illusory. Of course, our freedom is limited and our choices are always conditioned by various factors, such as our previous choices and our circumstances. But relative conditioning is a different matter from absolute determination.

The Confession in the following paragraphs unfolds the theological history of human freedom, and, following Augustine, it distinguishes four stages.

CF XI,2   Man, in his state of innocency, had freedom and power to will and to do that which is good and well-pleasing to God; but yet mutably, so that he might fall from it.

The first stage in the history of freedom is one that lies beyond the range of our experience. It is the freedom of sinless man. But such is the gravity of sin that it is scarcely possible for us to conceive the kind of freedom proper to a sinless man in terms of the only freedom we know in our experience, which is the freedom of sinners. The freedom of sinless man is described in the Confession as a freedom which is exercised in responsible obedience to God, and not apart from it; "in his state of innocency" man's responsibility coincides with his freedom. (Compare CF IV, 2.) But the discovery and isolation of the moment of freedom makes it possible for man to exchange the freedom of responsibility for the freedom of indifference, and so to lose it.

CF XI,3   Man, by his fall into a state of sin, hath wholly lost all ability of will to any spiritual good accompanying salvation; so as a natural man, being altogether averse from that good, and dead in sin, is not able, by his own strength, to convert himself, or to prepare himself thereunto.

Since the essential freedom of man consists in his responsible relation to God, man's choice of irresponsibility causes a breach in the relationship, which cannot then be mended by a mere reversal of his choice. A man who has broken his marriage by unfaithfulness cannot repair it at will; even though he should wish to do so, it is not in his power. It is the tragic paradox of sinful man that by the irresponsible misuse of his freedom he forges the fetters of his own enslavement. This does not mean that sinful man undergoes a psychological change, such as loss of freedom of choice or of strength of will in the ordinary sense of the terms, though these things may follow in extreme cases of self-indulgence. It is rather that by severing himself from God man sets himself adrift and becomes a different man, "a natural man," as the Bible and the Confession call him. (It should be noted that in modern English "natural" is often used in the sense of "essential"; in relation to this usage the natural man of the Bible is an unnatural or denatured man.) The man who has unmade himself in this way cannot remake himself in the image of his Creator.

CF XI,4   When God converteth a sinner and translateth him into the state of grace, he freeth him from his natural bondage under sin, and, by his grace alone, enableth him freely to will and to do that which is spiritually good; yet so as that, by reason of his remaining corruption, he doth not perfectly, nor only, will that which is good, but doth also will that which is evil.

The reconciliation of man to God by grace restores his freedom because it restores the relationship to which it belongs. God brings man back to a position in which he can resume a life of responsibility to God. God binds man to himself again and so sets him again under obligation to himself. But though man's enslavement to his sinful past is thereby broken in principle, he cannot in a moment undo what he has made of himself; he has to become the new man he now is in a continuing struggle with the old man he was. It is one of the paradoxes of the gospel that when man is reconciled to God he is divided against himself and daily called to do battle against himself. (Rom. 7.) To be called to freedom means to be called to join in the warfare of the Spirit against the flesh. (Gal. 5.)

CF XI,5   The will of man is made perfectly and immutably free to good alone, in the state of glory only.

The hope which sustains the Christian in the warfare of freedom is the final attainment of a state in which freedom is perfected in a constancy from which all risk of falling away is removed. This is the supreme paradox of the Christian gospel, that it looks to a consummation in which the age-old dispute between freedom and necessity is finally resolved in a happy marriage.

■ chapter XII[1]

OF EFFECTUAL CALLING

CF XII,1   All those whom God hath predestinated unto life, and those only, he is pleased, in his appointed and accepted time, effectually to call, by his word and Spirit, out of that state of sin and death in which they are by nature, to grace and salvation by Jesus Christ: enlightening their minds, spiritually and savingly, to understand the things of God, taking away their heart of stone, and giving unto them an heart of flesh; renewing their wills, and by his almighty power determining them to that which is good; and effectually drawing them to Jesus Christ; yet so as they come most freely, being made willing by his grace.

The Confession has already dealt with God's eternal purpose of salvation and with the publication of it in the gospel. It now turns to the communication and application of the gospel to men. In this and the following several chapters it sets forth what happens to the lives of men when they receive the gospel and it takes effect in them.[2]

----

[1] Chapter X in the Confession of Faith of the United Presbyterian Church in the USA.

[2] This series of topics used to be called the *ordo salutis* (way of salvation). They have been differently arranged by different authorities, and the order in which they appear in the Confession—calling, justification, adoption, sanctification, saving faith, repentance—is somewhat peculiar; faith and repentance would seem to be more appropriately placed at the beginning of the series rather than at the end. The series, however, was not intended to

The gospel of salvation is first presented to man in the form of a call. This is the gracious characteristic of God's dealings with man, that he makes his approach to him, not in the wind or the earthquake or the fire, but in the still, small voice; God respects the freedom he has given man and calls him to free, responsive decision. This call is addressed to man in the word and it becomes effectual in the power of the Spirit. Man's response to it involves his whole being—mind, heart, and will—and it brings him into a new personal relation to God in Jesus Christ.

CF XII,2   This effectual call is of God's free and special grace alone, not from anything at all foreseen in man, who is altogether passive therein, until, being quickened and renewed by the Holy Spirit, he is thereby enabled to answer this call, and to embrace the grace offered and conveyed in it.

Man's response to the call is itself the work of God's grace and does not arise from some capacity or potentiality inherent in man. Evangelical doctrine, in its proper concern to magnify the grace of God in man's salvation, may sometimes seem to reduce man to the condition of an inanimate object, like a pawn on the chessboard—and the use of the word "passive" in this paragraph points to that direction. But the real intention of the doctrine is to stress the magnitude of the transition from sin to salvation, which the New Testament compares to the transition from death to resurrection (Rom. 6:5-11; Col. 2:12); as the dead man is unable to raise himself, the sinner is in no position to help himself. When the sinner responds to the call of God, it means that he

---

be regarded as a sequence in which one item follows another in a strict order, but rather as various elements or aspects of one complex experience. Moreover, the elements specified here are only a selection from a wider range of terms which are used in the New Testament to describe the Christian experience, and some of which, such as regeneration and conversion, might well be considered to have as good a claim as the rest to inclusion in the Confession.

is already a new man and "is passed from death unto life." (John 5:24.)

CF XII,3   Elect infants, dying in infancy, are regenerated and saved by Christ through the Spirit, who worketh when, and where, and how he pleaseth. So also are all other elect persons who are incapable of being outwardly called by the ministry of the word.

This is one of the most controversial paragraphs in the Confession. Exception has been taken to it, not for what it says, but for what it implies, namely, that there are infants which are not elect and not saved. Attempts to deny that this implication is present cannot succeed; for it is logically involved in the doctrine of the "double decree" stated in CF III, 3. The paragraph, however, is not concerned with the question whether non-elect infants can be saved, but with the question how God's saving purpose can be effected with elect infants who die before they are old enough to receive and respond to the call of the word. The question also arises in connection with persons of mature age who through mental deficiency or other circumstance are incapable of receiving the call of the word. The Confession here applies the principle referred to in X, 4, that while the call of the word is "the divinely established and ordinary method" by which God effects his saving purpose with men, he is free to dispense with the call of the word and save men by the extraordinary method of the Spirit alone. But this does not mean that *we* can dispense with the ministry of the word; the exception proves the rule.

CF XII,4   Others, not elected, although they may be called by the ministry of the word, and may have some common operations of the Spirit, yet they never truly come to Christ, and therefore cannot be saved: much less can men, not professing the Christian religion, be saved in any other way whatsoever, be they never so diligent to frame their lives according to the light of nature,

> and the law of that religion they do profess; and to
> assert and maintain that they may is without warrant
> of the word of God.

The freedom of God to effect his saving purpose by extraordinary methods in extraordinary cases, which is invoked in
Paragraph 3, is here extended in an opposite direction, where it
assumes a rather dubious form. The extraordinary cases cited
here are those in which the call of the word and/or the operation
of the Spirit, or its equivalent, are present, but no possibility of
salvation is allowed. This is to reduce the freedom of grace to
sheer caprice. It is difficult to see how the authors of the Confession could maintain that there are people who respond to the
call of the word and experience the work of the Spirit and yet
cannot be saved, in view of Paul's emphatic assertion that "the
gifts and the call of God are irrevocable." (Rom. 11:29, RSV.) With
regard to the second group, who are described as "not professing
the Christian religion" (this ambiguous phrase is evidently intended to refer to people of other religions—Buddhists, Moslems,
and the like—who dwell in lands where the word has not been
heard, rather than to people in Christendom who hear and reject
the call of the word), it is difficult to see why the absence of a
Christian profession should be held against them, since the same
is true presumably of the persons referred to in Paragraph 3 who
can be saved without the outward call of the word. The final
statement that there is no Scriptural warrant for asserting that
"good pagans" can be saved surely overlooks Romans 2.

The paragraph illustrates the fact that a doctrine of predestination which refers salvation ultimately to a secret and
inscrutable decree effectually undermines the assurance of salvation, which in CF XX is founded on the veracity of the word and
the evidential reliability of the work of the Spirit.

◼ chapter XIII[1]

OF JUSTIFICATION

CF XIII,1   Those whom God effectually calleth, he also freely justifieth: not by infusing righteousness into them, but by pardoning their sins, and by accounting and accepting their persons as righteous; not for anything wrought in them, or done by them, but for Christ's sake alone; not by imputing faith itself, the act of believing, or any other evangelical obedience to them, as their righteousness; but by imputing the obedience and satisfaction of Christ unto them, they receiving and resting on him and his righteousness by faith; which faith they have not of themselves, it is the gift of God.

Justification is the chief doctrinal issue which divided the church at the Reformation. Luther called it "the article by which the church stands or falls," because he saw that in it nothing less than the gospel itself was at stake. The question at issue behind the conflict between the Roman and the evangelical interpretations of justification was whether the church was to hold firm to the gospel of Christ or abandon it for another, which is no gospel. (Gal. 1:6-7.) The evangelical doctrine of justification takes us to the heart of the gospel.

The statement of the evangelical doctrine in Paragraph 1 contrasts it at several points with the Roman understanding of it. The difference between them is due, in part, to a linguistic

---

1 Chapter XI in the Confession of Faith of the United Presbyterian Church in the USA.

factor. The term "justify" is derived from the Latin word, *justificare*, which was used in the Bible of the medieval church to render the Greek word, *dikaioun*, which is used in the New Testament (for example, Romans 3:24). *Justificare* means literally "to make righteous," and it was understood in this sense by those who read the New Testament in Latin. The message of the New Testament that sinners are justified freely by the grace of God was taken to mean that they are actually changed from sinners into righteous men, and the grace of God was understood as a supernatural force which effects this change by infusing into them some incipient or rudimentary righteousness, or some quality or disposition that could be considered meritorious. Since righteousness is a quality which is ordinarily acquired by the performance of righteous acts, and these are ruled out in the case of sinners, justification was thought to mean that God actually imparts to them the quality which corresponds to the acts, even though the acts had not been done; but since it was extremely difficult to think of any man as possessing a quality which he had done nothing to merit, it naturally came to be thought that God justifies sinners on the prospect of future performance; and it was but a short step to the notion that justification itself is a gradual process which is accomplished when the sinner is actually transformed into a righteous man by the performance of righteous acts. But it is easy to see that in this form the doctrine is barely distinguishable from the doctrine of justification by the works of the law, and there is no *gospel* about it for the sinner who is tormented by the sense of his own inability to do good works.

It was such torment that drove Luther to the study of the Epistle to the Romans and led him to the discovery that justification in the New Testament sense of the term does not mean that God makes the sinner into a righteous man but that he forgives him his sin; righteousness is not imparted to the sinner as a quality which he can possess in himself, but it is imputed to him as a free gift of grace. God justifies sinners "by pardoning their sins, and by accounting and accepting their persons as righteous," not because the works they have done, or will do, are actually

righteous. But does this not involve God in a fiction? How can
sinners be accounted righteous in their persons if there is no
actual righteousness to which they can point? The answer is that
the righteousness of justified sinners is not to be looked for in
themselves; it is the righteousness of Christ, and it is theirs as they
receive and rest on him and his righteousness by faith. The
consequence, as Luther was fond of saying, is that the justified
sinner is in the paradoxical condition of being a righteous man
and a sinner at the same time; considered in himself, in respect
of the qualities of his own life, he is a sinner, but in Christ—i.e.,
in the relation to Christ in which he stands by faith—he is a
righteous man, for he is accepted for Christ's sake. The evangelical doctrine of justification expresses the heart of the gospel—
that he who accepts Christ is accepted.

CF XIII,2   Faith, thus receiving and resting on Christ and his
               righteousness, is the alone instrument of justification;
               yet is it not alone in the person justified, but is ever
               accompanied with all other saving graces, and is no
               dead faith, but worketh by love.

The all-important word in this paragraph is "alone." Luther
in his German Bible added this word to the phrase "justified by
faith" in Romans 3:28, and was much criticized by his opponents
for taking liberties with the text. They contended that it was
absurd to suppose that a man could be justified "by faith alone"
or "mere faith," which, as they thought, or pretended to think,
meant that a man is justified merely by believing he is justified—
an interpretation which would bring it into the category of what
is now called "wishful thinking"; they argued that a man can be
justified only by a faith that is fully formed and developed by the
performance of works of love. The paragraph defines the evangelical doctrine in face of these two criticisms. First, it repeats the
truth, already shown in Paragraph 1, that the faith, by which
alone a man is justified, is not a species of auto-suggestion but a
receiving and resting on Christ and his righteousness; in other
words, it is an act in which a man turns away from himself and

places his entire reliance on Christ. Secondly, it states that when a man so receives Christ in living faith, his faith will blossom into works of love; but these works are the consequences of justification, not the conditions. We are justified by faith alone, but when we are justified our faith will not remain alone. These two truths reflect the two complementary emphases of Paul and James—Paul, "that a man is justified by faith without the deeds of the law" (Rom. 3:28), and James, that "faith, if it hath not works, is dead, being alone" (James 2:17).

CF XIII,3   Christ, by his obedience and death, did fully discharge the debt of all those that are thus justified, and did make a proper, real, and full satisfaction to his Father's justice in their behalf. Yet inasmuch as he was given by the Father for them, and his obedience and satisfaction accepted in their stead, and both freely, not for anything in them, their justification is only of free grace; that both the exact justice and rich grace of God might be glorified in the justification of sinners.

The gospel of justification by faith has from its first publication been thought by some to be too good to be true. (Rom. 3:8.) There have been some among those most deeply concerned with righteousness to whom it has seemed that a righteousness imputed to us by free grace and received by faith alone is too risky and precarious a conception unless we can be convinced that somewhere along the line this righteousness, in which we are invited to rest, itself rests on a secure foundation. Normally a man feels that his title to righteousness is secure only if he has himself acquired it by meritorious action; and though, of course, this kind of security was ruled out in the doctrine of justification, so far as we are concerned, it was thought that there was a place for it in connection with Christ; that is to say, the righteousness of Christ, which is freely imputed to us and received by faith alone, was considered to have been *merited* by him by "his obedience and satisfaction," and in this way the faith that our debt was freely cancelled was made easier because it was combined with the faith that our debt had in fact been paid: "Christ, by his obedience and death, did fully discharge the debt of all those that are thus justified."

This ingenious combination of grace and merit was first made in the medieval church before the Reformation, and it corresponds closely to the view of the work of Christ which was propounded by Anselm. (Compare CF VIII, 5.) It is interesting to note that even then there were some who suspected that the conception had the effect of detracting from the sovereignty and sufficiency of grace, and they introduced certain modifications with a view to minimizing this effect. In addition to renewing the emphasis of Anselm that the whole arrangement whereby Christ paid the debt of our sin was instituted by the Father, some theologians advanced the view that Christ did not really pay the debt, in the sense of offering the exact equivalent, so that God was bound to honor the payment (as Anselm had taught), but that God merely was pleased to accept the obedience and death of Christ, which did not have sufficient value, as a kind of token-payment. The theory was thought to have the advantage of providing a way of reconciling the justice of God, which requires that the debt of sin be paid, and the grace of God, whereby he freely pardons sin; for it taught that while God freely cancelled the debt, he at the same time upheld the principle, or at least the appearance, of payment.

This theory was taken over by Calvin, who defended the position "that Christ is truly and properly said to have *merited* the grace of God and salvation for us." (*Institutes,* II, XVII.) The theory is reproduced in this paragraph of the Confession, and an attempt is made to indicate the relative parts of merit and grace in our justification. The claims of God the Father against sinful men (which are represented in terms both of debt and of justice) are fully met by Christ, who "did fully discharge the debt . . . and did make a proper, real, and full satisfaction to his Father's justice"; justification is thereby established on a solid foundation of merit (i.e., the merit of Christ). But since God's gift of Christ to do this work *for men* and his acceptance of it in satisfaction of his claims against them are in no sense merited *by men*, but are done "both freely, not for anything in them, their justification is only of free grace." Merit operates in the transaction between Christ and the Father, grace in God's assignment of the benefits of this transaction to sinners. Calvin reveals that there were some people in his day who suspected that this kind of attempt to strike a balance between "the exact justice and rich grace of God" obscured the sovereignty of grace, and he is at pains to refute them. But it is to be feared that their suspicions were well founded; for if God's grace is contingent on "a proper, real, and full satisfaction" of his justice, grace is not sovereign, and justification cannot be said to be "*only* of free grace." The retention of the conception of merit in conjunction with the doctrine of justification represents a carry-over from medieval catholicism and is barely consistent with the Reformers' evangelical rediscovery of the sufficiency of grace alone.

CF XIII,4   God did, from all eternity, decree to justify all the elect; and Christ did, in the fullness of time, die for their sins and rise again for their justification: nevertheless they are not justified until the Holy Spirit doth, in due time, actually apply Christ unto them.

CF XIII,5   God doth continue to forgive the sins of those that are justified; and although they can never fall from the state of justification, yet they may by their sins fall under God's fatherly displeasure, and not have the light of his countenance restored unto them, until they humble themselves, confess their sins, beg pardon, and renew their faith and repentance.

Justification is "an *act* of God's free grace" (SC 33), which is done once-for-all. It is the definitive, conclusive, irrevocable character of justification as an act of God that forms the foundation of evangelical faith. The act-ual character of justification is further reflected in the fact that it happens to us as an event in our experience, and indeed our justification is not really effected until it is appropriated by us in this way. Nevertheless, it is not from the fact that we may be able to point to the day on which we appropriated justification (the day of our conversion) that justification derives its evangelical character, but from the once-ness of the offering of Christ (Heb. 9:26-28), which expresses the finality of the justifying act of God (Rom. 8:31-39). To base faith on the event in our experience would be to build a house on sand; for the truth is that we continue to sin after the event, and we cannot be absolved of our sin by appeal to our former experience. The true evangelical depth of the gospel of justification comes to light in the paradoxical fact, which the Confession touches on here, that while justification is once-for-all, it can be renewed, and is, in fact, daily renewed, as the believer, who cannot pass a day without sin, daily seeks and receives the forgiveness of sins. To put this, however, as the Confession does, in the form that, though the justified sinner can fall into sin, he cannot fall from "the state of justification," is misleading if the state of justification is thought of as a condition resulting from the experience of justification. What is irreversible is the relationship which is established by the justifying act of God in Christ; "if we are faithless, he remains faithful." (II Tim. 2:13, RSV.)

CF XIII,6   The justification of believers under the Old Testament was, in all these respects, one and the same with
the justification of believers under the New Testament.

This point, which has been already mentioned in CF VII, 5 and 6, and VIII, 6, is particularly important in connection with the doctrine of justification, because some of the language used by Paul to point the contrast between grace and law seems to imply an absolute contrast between the New Testament and the Old, as if the former represented the religion of grace and the latter the religion of law, and as if those who lived before the advent of Christ had no option but to seek righteousness by the law. This, however, is only one aspect of his teaching, and when it is viewed in the context of his teaching on this subject as a whole, it becomes clear that when Paul contrasts the gospel of grace with the religion of the law, it is not the religion of the Old Testament he means, but the religion of the synagogue, in which, as he puts it, the Book of the Law is read by people having a veil over their minds so that its true meaning does not get through to them. (II Cor. 3.) The legalism of the synagogue is a misunderstanding of the original intention of the law, which is to bear witness to grace (Rom. 3:21) and prepare the way for its coming (Gal. 3:23-24). Paul appeals beyond the legalism of the synagogue to the authentic religion of the Old Testament, which is the religion of grace, and he repeatedly cites Abraham as the prototype and supreme example of a man justified by faith. (Rom. 4; Gal. 3.) The publication of the gospel of Christ marks, not the reversal, but the fulfillment of the religion of the Old Testament. (Matt. 5:17.)

■ chapter XIV[1]

OF ADOPTION

CF XIV,1   All those that are justified, God vouchsafeth, in and for his only Son Jesus Christ, to make partakers of the grace of adoption: by which they are taken into the number, and enjoy the liberties and privileges of the children of God; have his name put upon them; receive the Spirit of adoption; have access to the throne of grace with boldness; are enabled to cry, Abba, Father; are pitied, protected, provided for, and chastened by him as by a father; yet never cast off, but sealed to the day of redemption, and inherit the promises, as heirs of everlasting salvation.

Faith, which was described in connection with the doctrine of justification as "receiving and resting on him [Christ] and his righteousness," means thus entering into a new personal relationship to God. The nature of this new relationship, which is enjoyed by justified sinners, is the theme of the doctrine of adoption. Adoption is not, therefore, to be thought of as something that follows justification. In SC 32 justification, adoption, and sanctification are grouped together as benefits of which "they that are effectually called do in this life partake"; they are best thought of as different aspects, or sides, of the same thing. In the New Testament Paul presents the heart of the gospel in terms of

---

1 Chapter XII in the Confession of Faith of the United Presbyterian Church in the USA.

justification by faith; John, who never speaks of justification, presents it in terms of divine sonship (John 1:12; I John 3:1)— which Paul also uses sometimes (Rom. 8:14; Gal. 4:5). Both mean the same thing; only, they present it in different pictures. Justification is a presentation of the gospel in "forensic" terms. The picture it suggests is that of a court of law in which a prisoner stands charged with an offense; the verdict is pronounced, "Not guilty," and the prisoner is discharged. Adoption is a presentation of the gospel in terms of family relationship. It suggests the picture of an orphan child, poor, hungry, and cold, standing outside the door of a warm and comfortable home; the door is opened, the child is taken into the family and surrounded with loving care. Justification concerns our responsibility to God and God's way of dealing with our failure to fulfill it. Adoption concerns our broken relationship to God and God's way of restoring it. Both pictures supplement each other, and they must be combined stereoscopically in order to provide a full view of the reality to which they refer. There has sometimes been a tendency in Protestant theology, especially in the Lutheran Church, to lean too heavily on the doctrine of justification. This is understandable in view of the decisive importance of the doctrine at the Reformation. But the fullness of the gospel is too rich to be compressed into the framework of this doctrine alone. For when God extends his grace to us in Jesus Christ, he not only releases us from our guilt, he also receives us into his family; and the one thing cannot be separated from the other without the risk of serious misunderstanding. The doctrine of adoption is sufficiently important to merit treatment alongside the doctrine of justification, and our Confession has the distinction of being the first in the Reformed tradition to accord it this recognition— even though the wording of the statement is exceedingly cumbrous, and, some have thought, barely grammatical!

"in and for his only Son Jesus Christ." It is through him who is Son by nature that we are enabled to become sons by adoption.

"the liberties and privileges of the children of God." Sonship, while it is a personal relationship, is also a legal status, a fact which enables us to see the close link between adoption and justification.

"have his name put upon them." That is, the Christian name, which they have "in Christ," as members of the family of God. This name, which is formally conferred on them at baptism, is different from the name which they bear as members of a human family, and which they have by birth.

"receive the Spirit of adoption." Sonship becomes activated in prayer, which Paul beautifully compares to that moment in the natural family when the infant child first tries to articulate the parent's name.

"are pitied, protected, provided for, and chastened." To be a member of the family of God means not only to enjoy his favors but also to come under his discipline. The effect of adoption is that a man's whole experience becomes a meaningful dialogue with God.

"yet never cast off, but sealed to the day of redemption." Adoption has a once-for-all character, like justification (CF XIII, 4), though the wayward child may feel rejection and the need of restoration. Adoption constitutes a binding relationship and one which points beyond its present reality to a fuller fruition, when our sonship will be perfected in the attainment of our eternal destiny.

■ chapter XV[1]

OF SANCTIFICATION

CF XV,1 They who are effectually called and regenerated, having a new heart and a new spirit created in them, are further sanctified, really and personally, through the virtue of Christ's death and resurrection, by his word and Spirit dwelling in them; the dominion of the whole body of sin is destroyed, and the several lusts thereof are more and more weakened and mortified, and they more and more quickened and strengthened, in all saving graces, to the practice of true holiness, without which no man shall see the Lord.

While justification, it was emphasized, is by faith alone, it was also made clear that faith is "not alone in the person justified, but is ever accompanied with all other saving graces, and is no dead faith, but worketh by love." (CF XIII, 2.) It is this constant accompaniment of justifying faith which forms the theme of this chapter; it deals with how the sinner, who is justified by "receiving and resting on him [Christ] and his righteousness," becomes possessed of righteousness "really and personally." The process is called sanctification, and the term is a reminder that the righteousness with which it is concerned is not established by reference to some abstract moral standard or ideal but is determined by a man's relation to God; for sanctification means

---

[1] Chapter XIII in the Confession of Faith of the United Presbyterian Church in the USA.

"making holy," and holy means "belonging to God." Fundamentally this is accomplished in justification, by which a man is released from the guilt which alienates him from God, and in adoption, by which he is admitted to the family of God. Sanctification is concerned with the manner in which the sinner, who by God's free grace is made to belong to God, becomes the kind of person who is fit to belong to God, not because he doubts his belonging to God by grace and prefers to earn this distinction by his own efforts, but by the transforming power of the relationship itself. The righteousness which becomes his in sanctification has its root in the righteousness which already is his by faith in Christ; for faith unites his life to Christ and brings it under Christ's direction and control "by his word and Spirit dwelling in them."

Sanctification, then, like justification, is not something we can accomplish by ourselves, but is a work of God's grace. It is appropriate that the verbs in which it is described in this paragraph are all in the passive voice. But this does not mean that sanctification is a process we undergo in a state of pure passivity, like a man undergoing an operation under an anaesthetic. The grace of God does not exclude our action, but, on the contrary, it calls us into action; for it admits us to a relationship which imposes an obligation upon us and summons us to obedience. When we are sanctified "really and personally" (not magically or mechanically), we are activated "to the *practice* of true holiness." We should not hesitate to put forth our utmost exertions in the pursuit of holiness from any fear of slighting the grace of God; the grace of God deserves our utmost exertions.

Sanctification is a gradual process. While justification is once-for-all, the character of sanctification is "more and more." For this reason it is appropriately defined in SC 35 as "the work of God's free grace," in distinction from justification which is defined as "an act" (SC 33). It consists in the gradual transformation of the sinner into a saint by his progressive emancipation from subjection to the sinful impulses of his nature and by his growing devotion and dedication to the new life to which he is called.

CF XV,2   This sanctification is throughout in the whole man, yet imperfect in this life: there abideth still some remnants of corruption in every part,[2] whence ariseth a continual and irreconcilable war, the flesh lusting against the Spirit, and the Spirit against the flesh.

CF XV,3   In which war, although the remaining corruption for a time may much prevail, yet, through the continual supply of strength from the sanctifying Spirit of Christ, the regenerate part doth overcome: and so the saints grow in grace, perfecting holiness in the fear of God.

Since sanctification is concerned with the renewal of man in the wholeness of his being and not merely with the amendment of some feature of his behavior, it is experienced in the form of inner conflict and struggle; for it sets a man at variance with himself and introduces a kind of civil war into his life. The contending forces in this war are described in Pauline language as the flesh and the Spirit. It must be carefully noted, however, that these terms do not refer to the two elements which are found together in man, the physical and the rational or spiritual; the conflict is not between the impulses of the physical and the aspirations of the spiritual. In the language of Paul "flesh" stands for the governing principle in the life of sinful man as a whole; and the lust of the flesh refers not merely to the bodily appetites but can be exhibited in the bent of the mind. (Rom. 8:5-8.) Similarly the Spirit refers, not to the spiritual element in man, but to the Spirit of God who is given to man and dwells in man as the principle of new life. The struggle is not between two elements *in* man, which he himself can distinguish (as Plato did), and over which he can set himself up as a kind of umpire; it is between two principles which contend for the control of his

---

[2] The use of the singular verb with the plural noun here may be cited as a minor illustration of the fallibility of synods and councils which is mentioned in CF XXXIII, 3.

being as a whole and between which it is not possible to strike an adjustment.

This conflict continues throughout this life. The Confession denies that the power of sin can be completely destroyed and perfection in holiness attained within the limits of this present existence. But it maintains that growth in grace is made possible by the hope of the ultimate attainment of perfection in the life to come. Sanctification, so to speak, is the current which flows between the two poles of grace and glory. (See SC 37.)

■ chapter XVI[1]

OF SAVING FAITH

CF XVI, 1   The grace of faith, whereby the elect are enabled to believe to the saving of their souls, is the work of the Spirit of Christ in their hearts; and is ordinarily wrought by the ministry of the word: by which also, and by the administration of the sacraments, and prayer, it is increased and strengthened.

Faith is a word which has several meanings. It can be used of the act or attitude of the person who has faith, the person who is the subject of the sentence, "I believe in God"; this is the *subjective* sense or aspect of faith. It can also be used to designate *what* a person believes, the object to which he refers when he says, "I believe in God"; this is the *objective* sense or aspect of faith, and clearly this is the sense in which the word is used in the title of *The Confession of Faith,* which is a statement of *what* the church believes, not just of how it behaves in the act or attitude of believing. This chapter of the Confession, however, is devoted to the subjective aspect of faith; it presents a description of what faith is when it is viewed as an act or attitude of the believing subject, or, in other words, it seeks to answer the question, What does a man do when he believes?

The theme is introduced in the first paragraph with a reminder that, though the subjective and objective aspects of faith can be distinguished, they cannot be separated. Faith is always in rela-

---

[1] Chapter XIV in the Confession of Faith of the United Presbyterian Church in the USA.

tion to its object; this is its nature, its origin, and its life. Though it has its subjective aspect, it is not something which the believing subject can generate spontaneously out of himself. Though it takes root in the heart of the believer, in the inmost depths of his subjective being, it is wrought there by the Spirit of Christ. Though it expresses his most personal conviction, it is elicited from him as his response to the word which is addressed to him. And its strength derives not from his strength of character, but from continued intercourse with its object, as it is represented in the "means of grace" (word, sacraments, and prayer; see SC 88).

CF XVI,2   By this faith, a Christian believeth to be true what-
            soever is revealed in the word, for the authority of
            God himself speaking therein; and acteth differently,
            upon that which each particular passage thereof con-
            taineth; yielding obedience to the commands, trem-
            bling at the threatenings, and embracing the promises
            of God for this life, and that which is to come. But the
            principal acts of saving faith are, accepting, receiving,
            and resting upon Christ alone for justification, sancti-
            fication, and eternal life, by virtue of the covenant of
            grace.

The Confession in this paragraph points to a further distinction of meaning which appears when faith is considered in its subjective aspect. It is usually expressed as the distinction between *assent* and *trust*. Faith as assent means believing that certain statements that are made are true; it is basically a mental act or attitude. "By this faith, a Christian believeth to be true whatsoever is revealed in the word"; that is, he gives his mental assent to the statements which he finds in the word, he holds them to be true statements. But, though this may be indispensable, it is obviously not enough. A man might give his full mental assent to the word, he might believe that every statement in it is true; but that would not make him a Christian, and it would be ridiculous to suppose that a man could be justified by such faith. Something more is needed, namely trust, which is described here as "accept-

ing, receiving, and resting upon Christ alone for justification,"
etc. The Confession calls these "the principal acts of saving
faith," and by this it indicates that the other act of faith, which
consists in believing certain statements to be true, is of lesser
importance. Faith as assent is preliminary or instrumental to
faith as trust; it is by itself nothing, but it is necessarily involved
or presupposed in faith as trust: "for he that cometh to God must
believe that he is." (Heb. 11:6.)

It is a question, however, to what extent faith as assent is
involved in faith as trust. While this question does not admit of
an easy answer, it seems clear that insistence on complete and
unqualified assent to the statements in the word as a principle of
faith would be incompatible with the relation between them
indicated in the Confession. Indeed, it is to be observed that the
Confession does not envisage a bare mental assent in the sense
of a belief in the veracity of the Scriptural record, but presumes
that this will be accompanied by an active response; and in
describing the different forms this response will take, it presumes
that the word takes the form of an address which demands an
appropriate form of response. Attention is confined to the commands, the threatenings, and the promises, but no mention is
made of the other things that are to be found in the word, such
as history, legend, and folklore, and no indication is given of
what the appropriate response of faith to such categories would
be. Assent to the veracity of the word does not preclude intelligent discrimination among its contents; on the contrary, some
capacity to distinguish between the kernel and the husk would
seem to be necessary if assent is to be crowned with trust.

At the same time, there is also a danger of exaggerating the
importance of trust, or "commitment," as it is often called in
modern speech, to an extent which obscures or denies the relative
importance of assent. This attitude occurs as a reaction against
an excessive emphasis on the intellectual element, but it is itself
excessive. It has appeared in its most extreme form in the philosophy of existentialism, which teaches that in a world where
there is no objective truth, man must seek his salvation by reso-

lute commitment to—whatever he chooses to commit himself to. It is also reflected in the attitude of those who say that it does not matter what beliefs a man holds in his head, so long as his heart is in the right place. How could his heart be there unless his head believes the place is right?

CF XVI,3   This faith is different in degrees, weak or strong; may be often and many ways assailed and weakened, but gets the victory; growing up in many to the attainment of a full assurance through Christ, who is both the author and finisher of our faith.

Faith, in the believer, varies in strength. It has to struggle with doubt and distrust. There are some whose faith grows to full assurance, but this is not granted to everybody. Yet even for those in whom the struggle with doubt and distrust is unremitting there is victory; for their faith is not in their own faith but in Christ, and from him it draws the strength to overcome.

■ chapter XVII[1]

OF REPENTANCE UNTO LIFE

CF XVII, 1   Repentance unto life is an evangelical grace, the doctrine whereof is to be preached by every minister of the gospel, as well as that of faith in Christ.

This should be read as a continuation of the theme of the preceding chapter; for faith and repentance belong together, like the two sides of a coin. Jesus began his public ministry by proclaiming the gospel of the kingdom of God and calling on men to "repent . . . and believe." (Mark 1:15.) The two things are inseparable. There can be no true faith without repentance; for faith means exclusive attachment to Christ and complete reliance on him, and, as such, it involves the detachment of all other ties that bind us, not only to sin but also to self: "If any man will come after me, let him deny himself, and take up his cross, and follow me." (Matt. 16:24.) But the two things constitute one indivisible movement of the self, and if repentance indicates the negative side of the movement and points to that from which the self turns away, it is worth noting that the Greek word for repentance in the New Testament means literally "a turning of the mind" and can be used also to point to the positive goal of the movement, as it is in the phrase which is taken from Acts 11:18 to form the title of this chapter, and which is obviously used there to include both repentance and faith.

There is a danger, however, that the inseparable connection

---

[1] Chapter XV in the Confession of Faith of the United Presbyterian Church in the USA.

of faith and repentance may not always be brought out as clearly as it should in the presentation of the gospel, and the Confession rightly calls the attention of ministers to their duty in the matter. It is a danger of which the apostle Paul was acutely conscious, as his moving address to the elders of the Ephesian church at Miletus shows; for in it he protests that he had "not shunned to declare . . . all the counsel of God . . . and . . . kept back nothing that was profitable . . . testifying both to the Jews, and also to the Greeks, repentance toward God, and faith toward our Lord Jesus Christ." (See Acts 20:17-27.) It is the danger of presenting the gospel in a manner which obscures or minimizes the radical and exclusive nature of the requirement of faith and which creates the impression that faith in Christ can be combined with faith in ourselves, or faith in America, or faith in democracy, or even faith in mammon. The gospel message is a summons to decision, not expansion; its key word is not Both-and, but Either-or. And when the gospel is faithfully preached, not only the attractiveness but also the costliness of faith must be made plain, if the fruit is not to be that partial and irresolute discipleship against which Jesus gave repeated warning. (Luke 9:57-62; 14:25-35.)

CF XVII,2   By it a sinner, out of the sight and sense, not only of the danger, but also of the filthiness and odiousness of his sins, as contrary to the holy nature and righteous law of God, and upon the apprehension of his mercy in Christ to such as are penitent, so grieves for, and hates his sins, as to turn from them all unto God, purposing and endeavoring to walk with him in all the ways of his commandments.

The motivation of repentance is a sense of sin, and by this is meant not merely a sense of the dire consequences which sin entails, temporally or eternally (for that would lead only to a prudential avoidance of sin), but a realization of the intrinsic sinfulness of sin, which produces an inward abhorrence of it and a revulsion from it. Such a realization can come to us only when we see our sin in the light of the righteousness of God, as it is exhibited in his law, and, even more, in his grace toward us in Christ; for it is one of the paradoxes of the gospel that the presentation of the mercy of God in Christ is the most effective means of leading men to repentance. Nothing can so open a man's eyes to "the filthiness and odiousness of his sins" so that he "grieves for, and hates his sins" as the assurance that his sins are forgiven. It is for this reason that repentance is sometimes spoken of in the New Testament, not as something which Christ demands as a condition of forgiveness, but as a gift which he imparts with forgiveness. (Acts 5:31; 3:26.) It is the presence of the holy love of God in Christ that moves a man to fall on his knees and say, "Depart from me; for I am a sinful man, O Lord." (Luke 5:8.)

If repentance is a gift of Christ, it is a gift which is realized in freedom. Indeed, it is the supreme act of human freedom; for in repentance a man breaks free from himself to make the venture of faith. It engages the emotions deeply, but is not only an emotion, like that sterile feeling of remorse of which Paul speaks (II Cor. 7:10); it engages the will and involves "purposing and endeavoring."

CF XVII,3   Although repentance be not to be rested in as any satisfaction for sin, or any cause of the pardon thereof, which is the act of God's free grace in Christ; yet is it of such necessity to all sinners, that none may expect pardon without it.

The relation between pardon and repentance is exactly parallel to the relation between faith and works which is set forth in CF XIII, 2. Repentance is not the condition of pardon, but the correlate. A man is not pardoned *because* he repents; but pardon is always accompanied by repentance in the man who receives it.

CF XVII,4   As there is no sin so small but it deserves damnation; so there is no sin so great that it can bring damnation upon those who truly repent.

The point of this statement is that the possibility of forgiveness does not vary in proportion to the magnitude of the sin committed, but is correlated with the presence or absence of re-pentance. The statement, however, raises two difficulties: (1) The first concerns the distinction between small sins and great sins. It is not easy to see how sins (as distinct from crimes) can be measured for size, since the most obvious and common-sense way of doing it was repudiated by Jesus in the Sermon on the Mount. (Matt. 5:21-28.) (2) On the other hand, Jesus drew a distinction which the Confession appears to have overlooked; while he extended the possibility of forgiveness to all manner of sins, he did make one exception, the sin against the Holy Spirit, for which, he declared, there is no forgiveness, neither in this world nor in the world to come. (Matt. 12:31-32.)

CF XVII,5   Men ought not to content themselves with a general repentance, but it is every man's duty to endeavor to repent of his particular sins, particularly.

This little piece of pastoral counsel which the Confession interposes here reflects a sapient awareness of some of the pitfalls which beset our path in this matter. One is the pitfall of "crowd psychology"; repetition of the General Confession or lamentations over the sinfulness of mankind are of no value unless the individual is conscious of his own personal sin. And since individuals differ, and each has his own besetting sin, it is their duty to examine their own lives and not

> "Compound for sins they are inclined to
> By damning those they have no mind to."[2]

CF XVII,6   As every man is bound to make private confession of his sins to God, praying for the pardon thereof, upon which, and the forsaking of them, he shall find mercy: so he that scandalizeth his brother, or the church of Christ, ought to be willing, by a private or public confession and sorrow for his sin, to declare his repentance to those that are offended; who are there-

---

[2] From *Hudibras* by Samuel Butler. (Volume I, Part I, Canto I, Line 215.)

upon to be reconciled to him, and in love to receive him.

This paragraph anticipates the doctrine which is more explicitly formulated later, in the chapters which deal with the church and the communion of saints (XXVII and XXVIII), namely, that the life of faith is a life in fellowship, and it points to the important place which repentance and forgiveness have in the Christian fellowship. Sin primarily concerns a man's relation to God, and, therefore, repentance, as was emphasized in the previous paragraph, is a matter for the individual, and it finds expression in his private confession to God. But sin and repentance do not belong exclusively to the vertical dimension of life, as we may call it; they also belong to the horizontal. We sin against our fellow men, and even against our fellow members of the church, and if we know what it means to receive the mercy of God when we repent and confess our sins to him, we "ought to be willing," in the power of the same faith, to repent and confess our sins to those we have offended, and they in turn to be reconciled to us and to receive us in love. The church is intended to be precisely the kind of community in which this is possible, a community in which the possibility of reconciliation, upon repentance and confession, is the very bond which binds its members together. (Rom. 15:7.) For the gospel is intended to operate in two dimensions, and to regulate not only the relations between man and God but also the relations between man and man. But this can only come about as the gospel induces an inward willingness in those who receive it, although, as the Confession indicates, this is not a reason why the practice of confession should not be given institutional form and regulation. The objection to the Roman Catholic confessional is not that it institutionalizes the practice of confession, with all that that implies in the way of formalization and constraint, but that it interposes the priest as a necessary intermediary between the confessor and God. While the doctrine of the priesthood of all believers disposes of the necessity of priestly mediation, it enhances the necessity of confession among believers, both to God and to one another; for when the church is no longer held together by the external cement of institutional structure and organization, there is the more need for the internal cement of reconciliation and love.

■ chapter XVIII[1]

OF GOOD WORKS

CF XVIII,1   Good works are only such as God hath commanded in his holy word, and not such as, without the warrant thereof, are devised by men out of blind zeal, or upon any pretense of good intention.

The word "good" appears to be one of the plainest words in the language, but when the question is asked what it means, especially when it is applied to "works," or actions, a number of different answers can be given. What is it that makes an act good? Probably the commonest answer would be that an act is good if it *does* some good, i.e., if it proves useful or beneficial to others. This view, which has been widely held, is known as utilitarianism. Utilitarianism teaches that the moral quality of an act is measured by its effect, so that the highest moral quality belongs to the act which effects "the greatest good of the greatest number." This sounds like common sense, and it can serve as a working principle in many matters of conduct. But it cannot take us all the way, and there is a point at which it clearly becomes dangerous; for it can be used, and has been used, to justify the sacrifice of the individual for the good of the nation as a whole. (See John 11:50.) The example of the totalitarian states shows that when morality is equated with utility, it all too easily degenerates into expediency.

Another common way of answering the question of what makes

---

[1] Chapter XVI in the Confession of Faith of the United Presbyterian Church in the USA.

an act good is to point to its motivation: an act is good if it is motivated by a good intention in the person who does it. This answer also contains some truth. The motivation of the agent (*Why* did he do it?) is certainly a factor, and an important factor in determining the goodness, or otherwise, of an action. It is superior to the answer of utilitarianism, inasmuch as it shows a greater consideration for the individual; and on that account it is more likely to commend itself to Christians—which may be why it is mentioned in the Confession. But here, too, there are obvious difficulties. An act done with good intentions may produce harmful results (to say nothing of the fact that an act done with evil intentions may produce good results). There is a general disposition among Christians and most people in the western world to respect the man who acts sincerely according to his lights, but the limitations of this as a moral principle are apparent in the familiar problem of the "well-meaning" person.

There are several other answers, which need not be mentioned here, except to say that their variety would seem to lend some plausibility to the view propounded by some, that there is no real answer, but only a convention; that is to say, there is no reason why certain acts are considered good, it is just that the generality of mankind have accepted the convention which calls these acts good.

The answer given in the Confession is that the good is prescribed for man by God. This is what marks it off as unique. All the other answers have this in common, that they assume that the answer is, or can be, given by man, that it is within his competence to judge and determine what is good. The answer of the Confession is that this falls exclusively within the competence of God: "He hath shewed thee, O man, what is good; and what doth the LORD require of thee . . ." (Micah 6:8.)

It seems clear that no other answer than this can be given, in view of the Christian doctrine of man. (CF IV, 2.) For if man is the creature of God, and if he was created for an eternal destiny in fellowship with God, if, in the words of the Shorter Catechism, his chief end is to glorify God (SC 1), the duty of man is determined by what God requires of him (SC 3). It should be noted that the sin of man is represented in the story of Genesis 3 as basic refusal to accept this definition of his duty, and this is why it has such momentous consequences; for man's sin is more than an isolated act of disobedience (as the relative triviality of the act itself shows), it is the rejection of a prescribed good for a self-chosen good (Gen. 3:6), and, as such, it is a denial of man's nature and destiny and an attempt to usurp the place of God (Gen. 3:5). The good for man is obedience to the commandments of God prescribed in his law. (See further Chapter XXI, Of the Law of God, which should be studied in close conjunction with this chapter.)

CF XVIII,2   These good works, done in obedience to God's commandments, are the fruits and evidences of a true and lively faith: and by them believers manifest their thankfulness, strengthen their assurance, edify their brethren, adorn the profession of the gospel, stop the mouths of the adversaries, and glorify God, whose workmanship they are, created in Christ Jesus thereunto, that, having their fruit unto holiness, they may have the end, eternal life.

If the good for man is prescribed by God in his law, as the first paragraph says, it would seem to follow that goodness consists simply in obedience to God's law. But moralists have objected that an act which is done in deference to the authority of an external law (they call this the principle of heteronomy), even if it be the law of God (theonomy), is not thereby good; for it might be done out of fear, or weakness, or blindness. An act is not really good, unless it is done freely out of the good will of the man who does it (autonomy). The Confession, however, sees no irreconcilable antithesis between the principle of heteronomy, or obedience, and the principle of autonomy, or spontaneity; for the goodness, which is the condition of doing the good works required by God, is itself the gift of God. This is the meaning of justification by faith: goodness cannot be acquired by the doing of good works, but the doing of good works is made possible by the goodness which God gives us freely, when he justifies us by faith and accepts our persons as righteous. (CF XIII, 1; XVIII, 6.) If believers can do good works, it is only because their goodness is God's work, and their works are a spontaneous response to his; "by them believers manifest their thankfulness, strengthen their assurance, edify their brethren . . ." Believers *are* good, through the work of God in Jesus Christ, and they are thereby set in the way of becoming good. By doing good works they *become* what they *are,* and they are headed toward the destiny for which they were created, when their goodness is crowned in holiness and eternal life in fellowship with God.

CF XVIII,3   Their ability to do good works is not at all of themselves, but wholly from the Spirit of Christ. And that they may be enabled thereunto, besides the graces they have already received, there is required an actual influence of the same Holy Spirit to work in them to will and to do of his good pleasure; yet are they not hereupon to grow negligent, as if they were not bound to perform any duty unless upon a special motion of the Spirit; but they ought to be diligent in stirring up the grace of God that is in them.

The goodness of believers, by which they are enabled to do good works, is spontaneous, but it is not self-generated. It is their spontaneous reaction to the work of God in Christ, and, as such, it is here ascribed to the work of the Spirit of Christ. As we have already seen in connection with the doctrines of justification and adoption, it is by the presence and work of the Spirit that the new relation of believers to God is realized in them subjectively. Hence, the spontaneity of the goodness of believers is not to be thought of in terms of a general disposition formed in them (such as we would call a Christian character), but "an actual influence of the same Holy Spirit." The spontaneity of believers is the spontaneity of the Holy Spirit, by whom they are actuated, and thus, paradoxically, it does not cease to be a spontaneity of obedience. It does not mean, as the Confession is careful to point out, that believers are to wait for a special motion of the Spirit before setting about their duty, as if they were relieved of their obligation of obedience. That obligation remains. The inspiration of the Spirit does not eliminate the perspiration of the saints.

CF XVIII,4   They, who in their obedience, attain to the greatest height which is possible in this life, are so far from being able to supererogate and to do more than God requires, that they fall short of much which in duty they are bound to do.

The Confession here points out the difference between the Roman Catholic and the Protestant teaching on good works, which is consequent on the difference between their respective interpretations of the doctrine of justification. (Compare CF XIII, 1.) In the Roman view, the doing of good works is indispensable to the justification of a man, and thus good works (which are done with the help of God) are held to be meritorious; that is, they are held to be capable of meeting God's requirement and procuring his verdict on the man who does them, by their intrinsic merits. This doctrine, in which good works are viewed as a kind of currency which God is legally bound to accept and honor, led inevitably to the development of a calculus or scale, by which the *amount* of good works required to procure a specific divine favor could be measured, and it even came to be thought that it was possible, by means of "works of supererogation," to do more than God requires and so to accumulate a credit balance with God, which could be disbursed (by the church) for the benefit of those who were not able to meet their obligations. This theory underlay the sale of indulgences in the medieval church and was challenged by Luther. The clearer apprehension of the righteousness of God and of the sinfulness of man (including justified man), which broke through at the Reformation, brought with it the knowledge that we are all permanently in God's debt. The best we can do falls so far short of what God requires of us that no man can hope by his good works to establish a credit standing with God; he can only pray:

"Suffice it if—my good and ill unreckoned,
And both forgiven through Thy abounding grace . . ."[2]

CF XVIII,5   We cannot, by our best works, merit pardon of sin,
or eternal life, at the hand of God, because of the great
disproportion that is between them and the glory to
come, and the infinite distance that is between us and
God, whom by them we can neither profit, nor satisfy
for the debt of our former sins; but when we have
done all we can, we have done but our duty, and are
unprofitable servants: and because, as they are good,
they proceed from his Spirit; and as they are wrought
by us, they are defiled and mixed with so much weakness and imperfection that they cannot endure the
severity of God's judgment.

CF XVIII,6   Yet notwithstanding, the persons of believers being
accepted through Christ, their good works also are
accepted in him, not as though they were in this life
wholly unblamable and unreprovable in God's sight;
but that he, looking upon them in his Son, is pleased
to accept and reward that which is sincere, although
accompanied with many weaknesses and imperfections.

The Roman Catholic doctrine of the meritorious character of
good works presupposes that the relation between God and man
is like that of two traders who do business with each other on
equal terms. The Confession here offers three reasons why this
doctrine is untenable. The first is that what God has done, and
will do, for us in Christ—forgiveness, reconciliation, and eternal
life—so far exceeds what we can do for him, even by our best
efforts, that there can be no thought of our procuring it by them;
it is ours only by God's free gift. The second is "the infinite

---

[2] From "At Last" (sometimes entitled "To Paths Unknown"), by John
Greenleaf Whittier.

distance that is between us and God," by which is meant, not spatial distance in the literal sense—for God is "not far from every one of us" (Acts 17:27)—but the difference between God the Creator, who has his being in himself, and us his creatures who have our being from him (compare CF VII, 1); we are essentially dependent beings, and it is impossible for us to reverse the roles and make God dependent on us, still less to place him in our debt. These two reasons, however, are still not enough to close the door against the doctrine of the meritoriousness of good works; for even if it be granted that we cannot by our good works procure a reward from God or indeed produce any effect upon him at all, the fact remains that God requires good works, and we are under obligation to perform them, and it seems to stand to reason that when we do them God will at least recognize them for what they are. The Confession rebuts this contention by recalling the point which was established in Paragraph 3, namely, that the goodness of any work we do is itself the work of the Spirit of Christ in us; and this goodness is always mixed with weakness and imperfection which arise from our own part in the doing of it. If then we want to have our good works appraised on the basis of what we of ourselves have contributed to the quality of them—and it would have to be this way if we stood in a trading relation with God—their value would be nil.

These three considerations would seem to add up to the conclusion that the good works we do are completely futile and worthless, and so to leave us wondering why we should do them at all. It is well known that, when the gospel message has been presented in the form of the doctrine of justification by faith and it has come home to the hearts of men with full force, some have felt that the doing of good works at all implied distrust of the sufficiency of grace alone and a relapse into the doctrine of justification by works. There were evidently some in Paul's time who felt that grace could be savored to the full only by those who renounced all concern for good works and chose to "continue in sin." (Rom. 6:1.) And similar ideas came up at the time of the Reformation, when the doctrine of justification by faith was renewed in the life of the church; there were some who held that the liberty with which Christ set men free (Gal. 5:1) included liberty from the obligation to do good works, and Amsdorf went so far as to say that good works were positively injurious to salvation.

The answer of the Confession to this difficulty is that the doctrine of justification, which, as previously defined, means the acceptance of the *persons* of believers (CF XIII, 1), and which, as is pointed out later (CF XXI, 5; XXII, 1-3), does not relieve them of their obligation of obedience to the law of God, extends also to their good works. That is to say, just as God in his free grace accepts the persons of believers as righteous, although they are in themselves unrighteous, so also by the same grace he accepts their works as good, "although accompanied with many weaknesses and imperfections," because they are done in the same faith by which those who do them are accepted through Christ. Believers are not only obligated to do good works and enabled to do them, but they are encouraged to do them by the assurance that, though they are always mixed with much that is not good, they are acceptable to God when they are offered to him as the active response of faith in his forgiving grace.

CF XVIII,7   Works done by unregenerate men, although for the matter of them they may be things which God commands, and of good use both to themselves and others; yet because they proceed not from a heart purified by faith; nor are done in a right manner, according to the word; nor to a right end, the glory of God; they are therefore sinful, and cannot please God, or make a man meet to receive grace from God. And yet their neglect of them is more sinful, and displeasing unto God.

This paragraph has been much criticized for what is considered its harshness and its inconsistency. It has been thought to be maintaining that "the virtues of the heathen are splendid vices" (a statement attributed to Augustine), and that, nonetheless, the

heathen would be in a worse case without them. A careful reading
of the paragraph will show that this is not its meaning.

The problem with which it is concerned is admittedly a very
difficult one. It has been called the problem of "the good pagan."
It might also be called the problem of accidental goodness.

It was pointed out in Paragraph 2 that the condition of doing
good works required by God is goodness which is the free gift
of God in Christ and which is received by faith. The problem
arises when we find works done which have all the marks of
goodness in themselves—they coincide with the specific require-
ments of God, they are beneficial to others, their motivation is
sincere—but they are done by men who have not received by
faith that goodness which is the free gift of God in Christ. Can
good works be done where the condition indicated in Paragraph
2 does not obtain?

The Confession does not deny, as it has sometimes been
thought to do, that these good works are in fact good. It merely
denies that they are meritorious, i.e., that they can satisfy God's
requirement or procure his favor. The Confession is here opposing a particular aspect of the Roman Catholic doctrine of good
works, namely, that while a man cannot do good works without
the aid of divine grace, he must first show some disposition to do
them in order to prove his worthiness to receive divine grace;
hence good works done by men before their regeneration were
deemed to have a certain provisional or preliminary merit. It is
the meritorious character of good works done by unregenerate
men that is denied here; and there is nothing startling about
this, since the same denial applies to all works, even the best
works of the regenerate. (Par. 5.)

Does this mean that pagans who do good works cannot be
saved? The Confession does not explicitly say so at this point—
perhaps because it has already said so in sufficiently explicit
terms in CF XII, 4 regarding "men . . . not professing the
Christian religion," who are, presumably, "unregenerate"—or
perhaps because it was felt that such a statement would be too
paradoxical altogether in face of the absolute obligation of all

men to obedience to God's will, which is reflected in the last clause of the paragraph.

"And yet their neglect of them is more sinful." The admission of degrees of sinfulness marks a lapse from the general attitude of the Confession and is hardly consistent with it. The Confession generally interprets the faith in terms of black and white; it draws a sheer and absolute contrast between the saved and the lost, between saints and sinners, which corresponds to the absolute and unalterable division between the elect and the reprobate. But there are some problems before which this all-or-nothing attitude breaks down, and the Confession is compelled to resort to the relativity of more-or-less.

■ chapter XIX[1]

OF THE PERSEVERANCE OF THE SAINTS

CF XIX,1   They whom God hath accepted in his Beloved, effectually called and sanctified by his Spirit, can neither totally nor finally fall away from the state of grace: but shall certainly persevere therein to the end, and be eternally saved.

CF XIX,2   This perseverance of the saints depends, not upon their own free-will, but upon the immutability of the decree of election, flowing from the free and unchangeable love of God the Father; upon the efficacy of the merit and intercession of Jesus Christ; the abiding of the Spirit and of the seed of God within them; and the nature of the covenant of grace; from all which ariseth also the certainty and infallibility thereof.

CF XIX,3   Nevertheless they may, through the temptations of Satan and of the world, the prevalency of corruption remaining in them, and the neglect of the means of their preservation, fall into grievous sins; and for a time continue therein: whereby they incur God's displeasure, and grieve his Holy Spirit; come to be deprived of some measure of their graces and comforts; have their hearts hardened, and their consciences wounded; hurt and scandalize others, and bring temporal judgments upon themselves.

---

[1] Chapter XVII in the Confession of Faith of the United Presbyterian Church in the USA.

The doctrine of the perseverance of the saints, which used to be considered one of the essentials of "Calvinism," is the logical consequence of the doctrine of God's eternal decrees in the form in which it is stated in Chapter III. If the latter is no longer acceptable in that form, the doctrine of perseverance is bereft of its premise. But it should not, therefore, be abandoned forthwith. In the discussion of Chapter III the endeavor was made to show that, though the doctrine of the double decree is built upon a misconstruction of the Biblical testimony, it was an attempt to give theological expression and form to a profound evangelical truth, which lies concealed behind its forbidding exterior. It is our task here also, in examining the doctrine of the perseverance of the saints, to seek for the kernel of truth which is contained in this husk.

The doctrine of the perseverance of the saints—which, it should be noted, does not say that the saints *ought* to persevere (though it is not excluded), but that they *will* in fact persevere—is, as we have said, the ultimate conclusion which must be drawn from "the immutability of the decree of election" (Par. 2); for if God has determined by a fixed and unalterable decree before the foundation of the world whom he will save and whom he will "pass by," and if the institution in time of all the means of salvation rests on this decree, it is unthinkable that any decree should be allowed to become a dead letter, and we are therefore compelled to conclude that those whom God has called, in virtue of the eternal decree, and who have set foot upon the path of salvation, will in the process of time "persevere therein to the end, and be eternally saved." They may, indeed, through their own frailty and perversity wander from the path and fall by the wayside and become, to all intents and purposes, abandoned sinners; yet it is a logical certainty that they will finally complete the course upon which they have entered.

The doctrine represents an attempt to establish the certainty of salvation on an objective basis, which is not dependent on the will of the saints. But since salvation is a process in which the saints are subjectively involved, it is not easy to see how this can be accomplished. The Confession tries to get around this difficulty by introducing the conception of a "state of grace," from which the saints, no matter how far they backslide (and according to Paragraph 3 this, it seems, can be quite far), "can neither totally nor finally fall away." By means of this conception the chain of logical necessity which links the eternal decree with the perseverance of the saints is completed. But this gain is dearly bought. For the real problem is not solved at all; it is merely split into two. The saints are left to ask the question whether they are actually in a state of grace (XX, 1), and the logical certainty, so far from relieving the psychological uncertainty, rather intensifies it.

It is a question whether this notion of a state of grace, which is of Roman Catholic ancestry, can have any place in an evangelical confession. To evangelical faith, grace is not a state which men can be in, without being aware of it, but a strategy in which God deals with men in personal encounter and response. The certainty of salvation cannot be taken out of this context and established on an objective basis as a matter of logical certainty. If the attempt is made, the effect is to change the nature of salvation from a dealing with men into a disposing of them; and this is inevitable if salvation is made to rest ultimately on the immutable and eternal decree. But since it is obviously impossible to exclude God's dealings with men from the picture altogether, the relation between his disposing of them and his dealing with them becomes a dark and tantalizing enigma. If the problem is split into two in this manner, the perseverance of the saints becomes meaningless, and the assurance of salvation impossible.

■ chapter XX[1]

OF THE ASSURANCE OF GRACE AND SALVATION

CF XX,1   Although hypocrites, and other unregenerate men, may vainly deceive themselves with false hopes and carnal presumptions of being in the favor of God and estate of salvation; which hope of theirs shall perish: yet such as truly believe in the Lord Jesus, and love him in sincerity, endeavoring to walk in all good conscience before him, may in this life be certainly assured that they are in a state of grace, and may rejoice in the hope of the glory of God: which hope shall never make them ashamed.

In the preceding chapter the Confession set up the doctrine that the ultimate salvation of those whom God has chosen according to his immutable and eternal decree is an objective certainty. It now turns to the question of how they themselves can become sure of this subjectively. The unhelpfulness of separating these two sides of the matter, which was pointed out in the discussion of Chapter XIX, now becomes more evident. It might have been expected that the subjective uncertainty of the saints could be resolved in a simple way by appeal to the objective certainty of their salvation previously established. But this is not the case. It now becomes clear that the objective certainty is of no help to the saints in their subjective uncertainty; on the contrary, it torments them, for it drives them on an anxious and

---

[1] Chapter XVIII in the Confession of Faith of the United Presbyterian Church in the USA.

sometimes agonizing quest for an assurance as firm as the certainty which belongs to their salvation, and that is not easy to come by when the only means available to them are of a subjective nature.

The first paragraph introduces the problem by pointing to the danger of a false assurance. The possibility of self-deception in this matter will be readily conceded; but how to detect it in practice—that is a different matter. The distinction between the hypocrites and other unregenerate men, who deceive themselves with a false assurance, and the true believers, whose assurance is genuine, sounds easy enough; but what if the true believers are in that backsliding condition described in CF XIX, 3? Will they not then be indistinguishable, not only by others, but even by themselves, from the hypocrites and unregenerate? The Confession mentions a number of specific tests which can be applied—genuineness of faith, sincerity of love, and conscientiousness of obedience—but since these tests (all of which really beg the question) must in the nature of the case be applied by believers themselves, who are obliged to act as judges in their own cause, believers are all too liable to find, when they begin to examine themselves—especially if they are aware of the capacity for self-deception that resides in the human heart (Jer. 17:9)—that they are sinking in a quagmire to which there is no bottom. When men interrogate themselves introspectively regarding the genuineness of their faith, the effect is likely to be that the assurance they crave slips further from their grasp.

CF XX,2   This certainty is not a bare conjectural and probable persuasion, grounded upon a fallible hope; but an infallible assurance of faith, founded upon the divine truth of the promises of salvation, the inward evidence of those graces unto which these promises are made, the testimony of the Spirit of adoption witnessing with our spirits that we are the children of God; which Spirit is the earnest of our inheritance, whereby we are sealed to the day of redemption.

The Confession moves here on to somewhat firmer ground. It indicates that assurance of faith comes, not from the result of an introspective examination of our believing, but from the divine truth in which we believe. Faith is most assured when it is least given to self-scrutiny; for faith is essentially a looking away from self to Christ, and when it turns its attention from Christ to itself, then, like Peter on the sea, it begins to sink. (Matt. 14:30.) This is the paradox of assurance, that, like happiness, it is most truly possessed when we are least concerned to seek it. The deliberate quest for assurance is thus apt to defeat its own object. But this does not dispose of our concern with assurance. It means only that we must go about it in a different way. This is the theme of the paragraphs which follow.

CF XX,3   This infallible assurance doth not so belong to the essence of faith but that a true believer may wait long and conflict with many difficulties before he be partaker of it: yet, being enabled by the Spirit to know the things which are freely given him of God, he may, without extraordinary revelation, in the right use of ordinary means, attain thereunto. And therefore it is the duty of everyone to give all diligence to make his calling and election sure; that thereby his heart may be enlarged in peace and joy in the Holy Ghost, in love and thankfulness to God, and in strength and cheerfulness in the duties of obedience, the proper fruits of this assurance: so far is it from inclining men to looseness.

The Confession rightly warns us against making assurance an essential element of faith, because to do so would be to make a law of assurance and to impose it as an obligation on believers, not only to believe, but at the same time to be sure that they believe. Assurance is not an obligation to be fulfilled, it is a gift which is bestowed, and for which "a true believer may wait long and conflict with many difficulties before he be partaker of it." It is not a gift which is bestowed as an exceptional addition to faith in some extraordinary way, like a bonus; it comes through the exercise of faith and the use of the ordinary means by which faith subsists. And this is the way in which it has to be sought; for though it is a gift, it is a gift which every believer is in duty bound to seek. As the believer perseveres in the exercise of his faith by the diligent use of the means of grace, in devotion to Christ, in obedience to his will, and in submission to the rule of his Spirit, assurance comes to him. But it does not come as a feeling which he enjoys when he contemplates his faith like a spectator; it manifests itself in a freer and fuller exercise of his faith. For assurance is, so to speak, a by-product of faith in action. As the Shorter Catechism puts it, it is one of "the benefits which in this life do accompany or flow from justification, adoption, and sanctification" (SC 36); that is to say, it is enjoyed when these things are actually taking place in our lives.

CF XX,4   True believers may have the assurance of their salvation divers ways shaken, diminished, and intermitted; as, by negligence in preserving of it; by falling into some special sin, which woundeth the conscience, and grieveth the Spirit; by some sudden or vehement temptation; by God's withdrawing the light of his countenance, and suffering even such as fear him to walk in darkness and to have no light: yet are they never utterly destitute of that seed of God, and life of faith, that love of Christ and the brethren, that sincerity of heart and conscience of duty, out of which, by the operation of the Spirit, this assurance may in due time be revived, and by the which, in the meantime, they are supported from utter despair.

It scarcely needs to be said that assurance fluctuates in strength, since the same has already been said of faith, which it accompanies. (CF XVI, 3.) The life of faith is anything but a life of ease and comfort and security; it is a life in which the believer is called to an unremitting struggle against the world, the flesh, and the devil, and it is no wonder that in face of such formidable foes he should sometimes be beaten back and have his assurance badly shaken. It is a gross distortion of the truth when the call of faith is presented to men as an invitation to a life of serene and confident mastery over circumstances. Rather, it is a call to battle against forces which contend for the possession of our souls and for which we are ourselves no match. (Eph. 6:12.) In this battle, periods of assurance will give way to periods of doubt and despondency, in which a man will feel himself driven to the brink of despair. If at such times the spark of faith is not utterly extinguished, it is not because a benign providence has arranged a rhythmic alternation of assurance and despair, like that of day and night, it is because at such times the believer is led into the innermost paradox of faith, which is that when it is weak, then it is strong. (II Cor. 12:10.) Luther, who knew more of the meaning of faith than any man since Paul, used to describe it as "confident despair"; for it is in the situation of despair that faith discovers its true strength. And Paul himself was able to go so far as to say, "I take pleasure in infirmities, in reproaches, in necessities, in persecutions, in distresses" (ibid.), because he knew that it is by the friction of faith against such things, so to speak, that assurance is generated.

To sum up, assurance is not something to be had apart from faith; it is not a guarantee that can be furnished by some independent testing agency prior to faith. Just as no man can have assurance of his ability to swim while he stands on the shore, but gains it only as he enters the water and commits himself to its sustaining power, so assurance comes to the believer only as he commits himself to the warfare of faith and learns the strength of the foes with which he has to contend.

▪ chapter XXI[1]

OF THE LAW OF GOD

CF XXI,1   God gave to Adam a law, as a covenant of works, by which he bound him and all his posterity to personal, entire, exact, and perpetual obedience; promised life upon the fulfilling, and threatened death upon the breach of it; and endued him with power and ability to keep it.

It was stated in the chapter which deals with creation that man occupies a special place in creation as the creature who is designed to respond to his Creator in free obedience (CF IV, 2); and this special relation between God and man, through which God's purpose with his creation is to be brought to fulfillment, is set forth in Chapter VII in terms of the covenant. The Confession now turns its attention to what it means for man to stand in this special covenant relation to God. It means that man is subject to the law of God. This is true of every man as man (Adam). As was noted in connection with CF VII, 2, there is no firm foundation for the existence of a covenant of works which is postulated as a precondition or presupposition of the covenant of grace. The point it is intended to express is that man, by his very being as God's creature, is under obligation to God.

CF XXI,2   This law, after his fall, continued to be a perfect rule of righteousness; and, as such, was delivered by

---

[1] Chapter XIX in the Confession of Faith of the United Presbyterian Church in the USA.

God upon mount Sinai in ten commandments, and written in two tables; the first four commandments containing our duty toward God, and the other six our duty to man.

Since the law is not an arbitrary burden imposed on man but is the only way in which he can be himself ("a perfect rule of righteousness"), it is not annulled by his failure to conform to it, any more than the laws of physical health are annulled by sickness; it remains the fundamental constitution of his being, and the giving of the law in the form of the Ten Commandments is interpreted as a republication of it in this sense (made necessary, as the Confession probably intends us to understand, by the fall of man). The distinction between the two tables of the law, which is made more explicit in Christ's summary of the law (Matt. 22:37-40), corresponds to the two principal elements in the structure of man's being, which were noted in connection with CF IV, 2, his relation to God and his relation to his fellow men. It may be observed that the law of God as it bears on the third element in the structure of man's being, his relation to the world around him, is not explicitly mentioned either in the Ten Commandments or in Christ's summary of them, and has to be sought elsewhere.

It was noted in CF VII, 5-6, that the giving of the law comes under the covenant of grace, since it is part of the work of God in bringing to completion his purpose in creation.

CF XXI,3   Besides this law, commonly called moral, God was pleased to give to the people of Israel, as a church under age, ceremonial laws, containing several typical ordinances, partly of worship, prefiguring Christ, his graces, actions, sufferings, and benefits; and partly holding forth divers instructions of moral duties. All which ceremonial laws are now abrogated under the New Testament.

CF XXI,4   To them also, as a body politic, he gave sundry judicial laws, which expired together with the state of that people, not obliging any other, now, further than the general equity thereof may require.

CF XXI,5   The moral law doth forever bind all, as well justified persons as others, to the obedience thereof; and that not only in regard of the matter contained in it, but also in respect of the authority of God the Creator who gave it. Neither doth Christ in the gospel any way dissolve, but much strengthen, this obligation.

While God's law is the fundamental determination of man's being, and is, as such, absolutely and permanently binding upon all men, it involves obligations which are relative to the concrete situations in which it has to be obeyed, and therefore distinctions must be drawn between different kinds of obligations, to which men are subject, and the different degrees of authority which they carry. This is especially evident in the case of the people of the Old Testament, who, because of the unique role they occupied in the history of God's covenant, were made subject, not only to the absolute and permanent moral law, but also to ceremonial and judicial laws, which were of relative and temporary obligation. The ceremonial laws consisted principally of ordinances concerning worship, the significance of which lay in their pointing forward to the fulfillment of the covenant in Christ, and they are connected with the provisional place occupied by Israel "as a church under age" in the unfolding purpose of God. The judicial laws were involved in the fact that Israel was at once a church and a state ("a body politic"), and they were necessary for the regulation of its life in its political aspect; since they were formulated in view of the peculiar historical conditions and geographical circumstances of the life of Israel as a primitive agrarian society, they are no longer obligatory, except in so far as they reflect general principles of equity.

The release of Christians from obligation to the ceremonial and judicial laws of the Old Testament does not mean, however, that they are left with nothing but their obligation to the moral law. Christians, too, are involved in obligations to different kinds of laws, not only moral, but ceremonial, judicial, and other kinds as well; and the problem of discriminating between them and determining the various degrees of authority pertaining to them is often one of peculiar difficulty. Thus, although most Christians today accept "the separation of church and state," they remain citizens, subject to the authority of the state, and it is not always easy for them to strike a balance between their political obligation to the state and their moral obligation to God. Similar problems may arise for them from their membership in the church, which must have laws for the regulation of its own life as an organized society. There have been times during which Christians have been constrained to defy the law of the church by their obedience to the superior authority of the law of God.

CF XXI,6   Although true believers be not under the law as a covenant of works, to be thereby justified or condemned; yet is it of great use to them, as well as to others; in that, as a rule of life, informing them of the will of God and their duty, it directs and binds them to walk accordingly; discovering also the sinful pollutions of their nature, hearts, and lives; so as, examining themselves thereby, they may come to further conviction of, humiliation for, and hatred against sin; together with a clearer sight of the need they have of Christ, and the perfection of his obedience. It is likewise of use to the regenerate, to restrain their corruptions, in that it forbids sin, and the threatenings of it serve to show what even their sins deserve, and what afflictions in this life they may expect for them, although freed from the curse thereof threatened in the law. The promises of it, in like manner, show them God's approbation of obedience, and what blessings they may expect upon the performance thereof; although not as due to them by the law as a covenant of works: so as a man's doing good, and refraining from evil, because the law encourageth to the one, and deterreth from the other, is no evidence of his being under the law, and not under grace.

CF XXI,7   Neither are the forementioned uses of the law contrary to the grace of the gospel, but do sweetly comply with it: the Spirit of Christ subduing and enabling the will of man to do that freely and cheerfully, which the will of God, revealed in the law, requireth to be done.

Although under the covenant of grace the fulfillment of God's purpose with men is not conditional on their obedience to the law, this does not mean that the law is of no significance to them; it continues to serve a number of purposes. The Confession here reproduces in summary the doctrine of the "three uses of the law," which was elaborated in the theology of the Reformers. (1) The law exhibits the authentic pattern of life for men, "informing them of the will of God and their duty." In this way it is of value to all men, and it serves as a guide particularly in the framing of political laws for the state. Hence this was sometimes called the political use of the law. (2) By exhibiting the requirement of God the law brings those who examine themselves in its light to a conviction of their own sin and their need of Christ and his salvation. This is what Paul meant when he said that "by the law is the knowledge of sin" (Rom. 3:20), and that "the law was our schoolmaster to bring us unto Christ" (Gal. 3:24). (3) The law continues to fulfill a function for those who have been brought to Christ and who have accepted his salvation ("the regenerate"), because the new life on which they enter involves an unremitting struggle against the old self (compare CF XV, 2), and the law serves, both as a deterrent to the remaining impulses of sin, and as an encouragement to persevere in the struggle against it. Though they know that their standing in the judgment of God is not determined by their obedience to the law, Christians will be glad to use the law as a guide and an incentive to the kind of life to which they are committed. They are doing nothing inconsistent with the gospel of grace when they use the law in these ways. The law comes into conflict with the gospel only when men think that by their obedience to the law they can become what God requires them to be. But Christians, who know they have become that by God's grace alone, still have to be what they have become—in other words, they have to live it out in their lives; and when they find uses for the law in this task, these are in no wise "contrary to the grace of the gospel, but do sweetly comply with it." For them the law is not a master whom they fear but a friend on whom they depend.

▪ chapter XXII[1]

OF CHRISTIAN LIBERTY, AND LIBERTY OF CONSCIENCE

CF XXII,1   The liberty which Christ hath purchased for believers under the gospel consists in their freedom from the guilt of sin, the condemning wrath of God, the curse of the moral law; and in their being delivered from this present evil world, bondage to Satan, and dominion of sin, from the evil of afflictions, the sting of death, the victory of the grave, and everlasting damnation; as also in their free access to God, and their yielding obedience unto him, not out of slavish fear, but a childlike love, and a willing mind. All which were common also to believers under the law; but under the New Testament, the liberty of Christians is further enlarged in their freedom from the yoke of the ceremonial law, to which the Jewish church was subjected; and in greater boldness of access to the throne of grace, and in fuller communications of the free Spirit of God, than believers under the law did ordinarily partake of.

Liberty, though highly prized, is often taken for granted by people who have not paused to reflect how complex a thing it is and how difficult are some of the problems it involves. The familiar statement of the Declaration of Independence, which

---

[1] Chapter XX in the Confession of Faith of the United Presbyterian Church in the USA.

names liberty among the unalienable rights bestowed upon all men by their Creator, presents a truth which no one contests, but it barely touches the practical question. The practical question is how men, who have the right to liberty, are to be able to exercise that right, or, in other words, how they are to acquire the capacity for liberty.

The immediate occasion of the statement in the Declaration of Independence was the invasion of men's right to liberty by an oppressive government, and the proximate goal to which it called them was resistance to the oppressor. This kind of liberty is called political liberty, and it is important enough in its own place, but it is by no means the whole of liberty, not even in the context of everyday life. It has become increasingly plain, for example, that political liberty brings little benefit without economic liberty, i.e., the liberty to engage in "the pursuit of happiness" without oppressive and disabling handicaps. But liberty has many aspects and dimensions beyond these.

In this paragraph the Confession summarizes the teaching of the Bible on the ultimate dimension of liberty. This goes deeper than freedom from oppression or freedom from want; it consists in freedom from sin, freedom from its guilt, its power, and its consequences, both temporal and eternal. This freedom is one of which men everywhere stand in dire need, and until they obtain it they are slaves, no matter what degree of political or economic freedom they may possess. All men are in this condition of bondage because they are alienated from God. It is not enough for men to be liberated from external restraints—for this might only mean being sold into slavery themselves. The real power of freedom, according to the Bible, lies, not in freedom *from,* but in freedom *for:* men are never truly free until they are free for God, free to devote themselves to him in faith and trust and willing obedience. But this is not a freedom they can achieve for themselves; it is the liberty of the children of God, the gift which God imparted to his people from the beginning of his convenantal relation with them and which is ours in its fullness through Christ.

CF XXII,2   God alone is Lord of the conscience, and hath left
it free from the doctrines and commandments of men
which are in anything contrary to his word, or beside
it in matters of faith or worship. So that to believe such
doctrines, or to obey such commandments out of
conscience, is to betray true liberty of conscience; and
the requiring an implicit faith, and an absolute and
blind obedience, is to destroy liberty of conscience,
and reason also.

The liberty of Christians, as we have just seen, is grounded in a
relation to God in which they freely and willingly acknowledge
his authority. It is when men come under the rightful authority
of God that they are set free. But this does not mean that they
are now free of obligation toward any other authority than that
of God. Both church and state, of which Christians are members,
involve the exercise of authority, and it is the relation of Christians to these authorities with which this and the following paragraphs deal. With regard to the authority of the church in matters of faith, worship, and discipline, the Confession deals only
with the case in which it comes into conflict with the authority
of God over the conscience of Christians. But this is not always
the case. Ordinarily the authority of the church does obligate
Christians, who recognize it as the means or instrument through
which God exercises his authority, as is indicated in Paragraph
4. The Confession proposes two tests to determine whether the
authority of the church is being used in that way or not. The first
is conformity to the word of God. Nothing that is contrary to the
word, or "beside" it (i.e., not found in it, like certain orders of
ministry or forms of church organization, which, though they
may be sanctioned by ancient usage, are without express warrant
in the word), can be held to be essential. The other test is liberty
of conscience (in the more restricted sense of the phrase). If the
church demands blind and unquestioning faith and obedience,
that is inconsistent with the authority of God, which can be
acknowledged only in freedom. God seeks of men the response

of free, willing, and trustful obedience, and no authority which requires slavish and uncritical submission can act as his instrument.

CF XXII,3   They who, upon pretense of Christian liberty, do practice any sin, or cherish any lust, do thereby destroy the end of Christian liberty; which is, that, being delivered out of the hands of our enemies, we might serve the Lord without fear, in holiness and righteousness before him, all the days of our life.

This paragraph states the familiar distinction between liberty and license, and indicates its basis. Liberty tends to degenerate into license when it is understood primarily in the negative sense of freedom from obligation, or when it is defined as freedom to do what you like. Christians know that they are not free at all until they are free for God, free to like what he obliges them to do. The opposite of freedom is not authority, but slavery. Freedom is possible only when it is happily married to true authority, the authority of God, whose service is perfect freedom.

CF XXII,4   And because the powers which God hath ordained, and the liberty which Christ hath purchased, are not intended by God to destroy, but mutually to uphold and preserve one another; they who, upon pretense of Christian liberty, shall oppose any lawful power, or the lawful exercise of it, whether it be civil or ecclesiastical, resist the ordinance of God. And for their publishing of such opinions, or maintaining of such practices, as are contrary to the light of nature, or to the known principles of Christianity, whether concerning faith, worship, or conversation; or to the power of godliness; or such erroneous opinions or practices as, either in their own nature, or in the manner of publishing or maintaining them, are destructive to the external peace and order which Christ hath established in the church: they may lawfully be called to account, and proceeded against by the censures of the church.

The Confession turns now to the more positive aspect of the relation of Christians to authority in church and state. Since these authorities have been instituted by God as instruments of his authority, Christians are in conscience bound to respect them; and resistance to legitimate authority in the name of liberty betrays a false conception of liberty and is to be construed as rebellion against God and punished accordingly.

With the principle set forth here there will be general agreement. But there are two things in this paragraph to which exception may be taken. (1) The proposition that men may be called to account for the publication of subversive opinions breathes a spirit of intolerance which is not cherished by Christians at the present day. It should be remembered, however, that the Confession was composed at a time when the power of ideas to influence action was greater than it is today. We live in an age of ideological inflation, when so many ideas are in the market that few of them are likely to endanger peace and order, and it has been deemed prudent to distinguish between "theoretical advocacy" and "incitement to action." (2) The Confession requires the obedience of Christians to *lawful* authority, *lawfully* exercised. Though it contemplates the possible abuse of ecclesiastical authority in Paragraph 2, neither there nor in Chapter XXV does it answer the question of what Christians are required to do when they are confronted with political authority that is unlawful, or unlawfully exercised.

■ chapter XXIII[1]

OF RELIGIOUS WORSHIP AND THE SABBATH DAY

CF XXIII,1   The light of nature showeth that there is a God, who hath lordship and sovereignty over all; is good, and doeth good unto all; and is therefore to be feared, loved, praised, called upon, trusted in, and served with all the heart, and with all the soul, and with all the might. But the acceptable way of worshipping the true God is instituted by himself, and so limited by his own revealed will, that he may not be worshipped according to the imaginations and devices of men, or the suggestions of Satan, under any visible representation or any other way not prescribed in the Holy Scripture.

CF XXIII,2   Religious worship is to be given to God, the Father, Son, and Holy Ghost; and to him alone: not to angels, saints, or any other creature: and since the fall, not without a Mediator; nor in the mediation of any other but of Christ alone.

This and the following chapter are devoted to "our duty toward God," which is contained in the first table of the law. (CF XXI, 2.) The word "worship" is thought to be a compressed form of worth-ship. It denotes the appropriate attitude and mode of behavior toward anyone of superior worth. (The mayor of an

---

[1] Chapter XXI in the Confession of Faith of the United Presbyterian Church in the USA.

English town is addressed as "Your Worship.") It is not limited to ceremonious acts of deference, which are only its formal expression.

The Confession begins by establishing a general basis for the obligation to worship in the facts of God's existence and universal sovereignty, as these can be apprehended in the light of nature. These facts are deemed sufficient of themselves to convince men that they ought to worship God; but in order to learn *how* God is to be worshipped, and to avoid error and superstition, they have to follow the ways prescribed in Scripture.

It is open to question whether the light of nature, which is said in CF I, 1 to be insufficient to give that knowledge of God and of his will which is necessary to salvation, can consistently be held to furnish a sufficient basis for the obligation to worship— although the fact that the impulse to worship would seem to be present in some form in virtually all men might be cited as evidence. But it is more than doubtful if the nature of Christian worship can be rightly understood if it is introduced as a specific manifestation of this general obligation to worship, regulated only by the prescriptions of Holy Scripture. Surely the worship which Christians offer to God, not as a duty only, but as a glad privilege, is the response which they make to the specifically Christian experience of salvation. This is implied in Paragraph 2 where it is said that worship is to be given to God the Father, Son, and Holy Spirit, and that it is to be given through the mediation of Christ alone. The worship which we offer to God in the name of Christ ought to be a reflection of what we know that God has done for us in Christ.

The prohibition of the use of visible images and mediators other than Christ points to the absolute distinction between God the Creator and all creatures. (Compare CF VII, 1.) Every attempt to bridge the gulf between them by the interposition of creaturely figures or to represent God to ourselves by means of creaturely images is to fall into superstition, the essence of which consists in blurring the distinction between God and man. When we worship, we must remember that "God is in heaven, and thou upon earth." (Eccl. 5:2.) We cannot cover the distance which separates us from God; but the basis of our worship is the fact that God himself in his grace has come near to us. We cannot represent God to ourselves by any image; but he himself is present with us in Christ through the Holy Spirit.

cf xxiii,3   Prayer with thanksgiving, being one special part of religious worship, is by God required of all men; and that it may be accepted, it is to be made in the name of the Son, by the help of his Spirit, according to his will, with understanding, reverence, humility, fervency, faith, love, and perseverance; and, if vocal, in a known tongue.

cf xxiii,4   Prayer is to be made for things lawful, and for all sorts of men living, or that shall live hereafter; but not for the dead.

Of the elements comprised in worship the Confession treats first of prayer. The word and the sacraments are dealt with in Paragraph 5. Both the Catechisms take them in another order—word, sacraments, and prayer; and this is probably to be preferred, as the word and the sacraments have to do with the proclamation and presentation of God's saving acts, to which prayer is the response. The Confession introduces prayer first, evidently because it seeks to relate Christian prayer, as it did Christian worship, to a more general obligation and impulse; but it is a question whether the distinctive nature of Christian prayer is not obscured in this way. The Bible recognizes the virtual universality of prayer, even among the heathen; but it does not introduce Christian prayer as a variation of heathen prayer. On the contrary, the first lesson we have to learn, when we enter Christ's school of prayer, is not to do as the heathen do. (Matt. 6:7.)

The interior aspect of prayer as the expression of the relation to which we are admitted as sons of God has been already dealt with in the chapter on adoption. (CF XIV.) The present paragraphs are concerned more with the regulation of prayer. The association of prayer with thanksgiving illustrates the fact that prayer is primarily acknowledgment of what God has done. This is the ground of the confidence with which we present our petitions; for "he that spared not his own Son, but delivered him up for us all, how shall he not with him also freely give us all things?" (Rom. 8:32.) The point of the prescriptions at the end of Paragraph 3 is that prayer is not a magical device but an intelligent act in which mind, heart, and will are fully engaged.

Paragraph 4 deals with the scope of prayer. We are to pray for all our legitimate needs—not only those which might be labeled as specifically religious—and for all sorts and conditions of men; and in so doing we serve as instruments of the saving purpose of God with his whole creation. The Confession, however, imposes one limitation. The prohibition of prayers for the dead is connected with the denial of any intermediate state between this life and the life to come. (CF XXXIV, 1.) The position taken is that every man's destiny is finally sealed at his death and that thereafter he is beyond both the need and the range of human prayers. Roman Catholics take a different view, and some Protestants have felt that prayer for those who have gone before would be a natural and proper expression of the communion of saints (CF XXVIII), which unites us not only with those now living but with all "that have been, are, or shall be gathered into one, under Christ" (CF XXVII, 1). While no one would condemn the loving concern that prompts such prayers, they are incompatible with evangelical faith, which accepts the finality of death because the gospel itself hinges on the finality of the death of Christ: "as it is appointed unto men once to die, but after this the judgment: so Christ was once offered to bear the sins of many." (Heb. 9:27-28.)

CF XXIII,5   The reading of the Scriptures with godly fear; the sound preaching, and conscionable hearing of the word, in obedience unto God with understanding, faith, and reverence; singing of psalms with grace in the heart; as, also, the due administration and worthy receiving of the sacraments instituted by Christ; are

> all parts of the ordinary religious worship of God:
> besides religious oaths, and vows, solemn fastings, and
> thanksgivings upon special occasions; which are, in
> their several times and seasons, to be used in an holy
> and religious manner.

The word and the sacraments are those elements of worship
which represent the saving acts of God in Christ. By the reading
and preaching of the word the gospel, the good news of salvation,
is proclaimed and, in being proclaimed, is realized, through the
Holy Spirit, as the power of God unto salvation; for the word is
not only a record of what God did and said once, it is the instrument through which he speaks to us and acts on us. That is why
the Confession stresses our hearing as well as the reading and
preaching of the word; by "conscionable hearing" is meant a
hearing in which we expose ourselves to the word with openness,
expectancy, and concern, and participate in it with our whole
being. The sacraments, which are associated with the word as
means of grace, are added because what God has done and does
and will do for us is greater than can be expressed in words (see
CF XXIX); and this is reflected also in that part of worship
which expresses our response to the gospel as it is presented in
word and sacraments; for here, too, words alone are inadequate,
and we are moved to sing.

While these form the ordinary and regular elements of worship, the Confession allows for special elements to meet the needs
of special occasions. Such variations will become significant acts
of communion with God and avoid the risk of becoming ceremonious occasions if they are in fact variations in a sustained
practice of ordinary worship.

CF XXIII,6   Neither prayer, nor any other part of religious wor-
               ship, is now, under the gospel, either tied unto, or made
               more acceptable by, any place in which it is performed,
               or towards which it is directed: but God is to be
               worshipped everywhere in spirit and in truth; as in
               private families daily, and in secret each one by him-

> self, so more solemnly in the public assemblies, which
> are not carelessly or willfully to be neglected or for-
> saken, when God, by his word or providence, calleth
> thereunto.

Worship is communion with God. It consists in the representation of God's saving acts in word and sacraments and our response in praise and prayer. As such, it is not restricted to any
location, but can be performed anywhere. This, of course, does
not preclude the erection and setting apart of special buildings
for the worship of the congregation, but it points up the danger
that if our worship becomes associated exclusively with such
buildings and we become dependent upon their architectural
features to induce the mood of worship, we may be diverted
from the worship of God in spirit and in truth; for this is not
a mood induced in us by soaring Gothic arches "And storied
windows richly dight, Casting a dim religious light,"[2] but is an
intelligent and adoring celebration of his gospel. The Confession
rightly introduces public worship in the context of family and
private worship, apart from which it is liable to become an empty
formality or a sedate kind of entertainment.

CF XXIII,7   As it is of the law of nature that, in general, a due
proportion of time be set apart for the worship of
God; so, in his word, by a positive, moral, and perpetual commandment, binding all men in all ages, he
hath particularly appointed one day in seven for a
Sabbath, to be kept holy unto him: which, from the
beginning of the world to the resurrection of Christ,
was the last day of the week; and, from the resurrection
of Christ, was changed into the first day of the week,
which in Scripture is called the Lord's day, and is to be
continued to the end of the world as the Christian
Sabbath.

---

[2] From "Il Penseroso" by John Milton.

CF XXIII,8   This Sabbath is then kept holy unto the Lord when men, after a due preparing of their hearts, and ordering of their common affairs beforehand, do not only observe an holy rest all the day from their own works, words, and thoughts about their worldly employments and recreations; but also are taken up the whole time in the public and private exercises of his worship, and in the duties of necessity and mercy.

As we can worship God in any place, we can worship him also at any time. "Evening, and morning, and at noon, will I pray, and cry aloud." (Ps. 55:17.) But a thing that can be done at any time runs the risk of being done at no time; and for this reason it is well that there should be a set time for worship—perhaps also because time is more restricted for us than space. When the Confession traces the propriety of this arrangement to the law of nature, the thought is probably of the nature of time, which is experienced by us not as an even and unvarying sequence but in the rhythmic alternation of day and night, summer and winter, seedtime and harvest, and which prescribes the pattern for our lives with its alternation of waking and sleeping, work and rest, and so forth. But the requirement of a set time for worship is more firmly based on the specific divine commandment which has appointed one day in seven to be a holy Sabbath. In the fourth commandment the institution of the Sabbath is related to God's rest on the seventh day after completing the six days' work of creation. The fact that God is said to have blessed the Sabbath day and hallowed it signifies that this day marks the inauguration of the reciprocal relation between the Creator and the creature. Having completed the days of creation, God now appoints a day in which he is free *for* creation, and he invites creation to participate with him in it. The invitation is addressed primarily to man, though it is extended also to cattle, who are privileged to enjoy its benefit in their own way. On this day man is called to be free for God, and to this end he is set free *from* the world, free from the toil and care of worldly existence. (Note how the motif of liberation from enslavement appears in the parallel version of the commandment in Deuteronomy 5:12-15.) But the humanitarian provision of release from toil, though it is important enough, cannot be separated from the more positive purpose of the day, which is the provision of a regular opportunity for the worship of God. The connection between them is enshrined in the beautiful phrase, "an holy rest," which points to a blending of rest that is holy with holiness that is restful. Concentration on the negative aspect of the Sabbath as the day of no work led to some of the worst excesses of Jewish legalism. This is not to say that exception need be taken to legal measures for securing the humanitarian purpose of the day. Yet, what men do not do on the Sabbath is never so important as what they do.

The Sabbath law of the Old Testament is not binding on Christians, who are not under the law. Yet the basic intention of the Sabbath as a day on which men are set free for God is more fully realized for Christians, who celebrate the resurrection of Christ as the supreme act of liberation. The substitution of the first day of the week for the seventh as "the Christian Sabbath" did not take place immediately after the resurrection, as the language of the Confession might be taken to suggest. The change was gradual, and the observance of Sunday was made official by an enactment of Constantine, the first Christian emperor, in A.D. 321.

▪ chapter XXIV[1]

OF LAWFUL OATHS AND VOWS

CF XXIV,1   A lawful oath is a part of religious worship, wherein upon just occasion, the person swearing solemnly calleth God to witness what he asserteth or promiseth; and to judge him according to the truth or falsehood of what he sweareth.

CF XXIV,2   The name of God only is that by which men ought to swear, and therein it is to be used with all holy fear and reverence; therefore to swear vainly or rashly by that glorious and dreadful name, or to swear at all by any other thing, is sinful, and to be abhorred. Yet, as, in matters of weight and moment, an oath is warranted by the word of God, under the New Testament, as well as under the Old, so a lawful oath, being imposed by lawful authority, in such matters ought to be taken.

CF XXIV,3   Whosoever taketh an oath ought duly to consider the weightiness of so solemn an act, and therein to avouch nothing but what he is fully persuaded is the truth. Neither may any man bind himself by oath to anything but what is good and just, and what he believeth so to be, and what he is able and resolved to perform. Yet it is a sin to refuse an oath touching

---

1 Chapter XXII in the Confession of Faith of the United Presbyterian Church in the U.S.A.

anything that is good and just, being imposed by lawful authority.

CF XXIV,4   An oath is to be taken in the plain and common sense of the words, without equivocation or mental reservation. It cannot oblige to sin; but in anything not sinful, being taken, it binds to performance, although to a man's own hurt: nor is it to be violated, although made to heretics or infidels.

The specific theme of this chapter is likely to be of only limited interest at the present day, when oaths are required to be taken only on rare occasions, such as the appearance of witnesses in a court of law or the assumption of office by public officials—and even then they tend to be treated in a formal and perfunctory way—and the making of vows (apart from marriage vows) is practically obsolete. The matter was of much greater concern at the time the Confession was composed, partly because of the predominantly legal temper of the age, and partly because many people were troubled in conscience over the propriety of oath-taking by Christians at all in view of the express prohibitions against it in the New Testament. (Matt. 5:33-37; James 5:12.) The passages are cited in the Scripture references to Paragraph 2 of this chapter in support of the prohibition of *vain* or *rash* swearing only; but this is a forced interpretation. The principle of liberty of conscience, enunciated in CF XXII, 2, could surely be invoked by those who read the passages as an absolute prohibition of oaths of any kind, and their right to do so is now generally respected in modern states.

The matter of oaths and vows, however, is only the focal point of a much larger issue, which is nothing less than the fundamental character of the Christian life. The life to which Christians are called is a life in response to the saving work of God in Christ, and its salient characteristic may therefore be described as responsibility. Oaths and vows merely afford pointed illustrations of the nature of Christian responsibility.

Christians are what they are by the grace of God. By their acceptance of the work of God in Christ they receive a new standing with God, and they are brought under an absolute obligation to respond by a way of life in relation both to God and to their fellow men. It is the powerful sense of this obligation which has led some to repudiate the taking of oaths by Christians; for they regard it as the responsibility of Christians to be the kind of persons whose word can be believed and relied on without the need of oaths. And in the ordinary speech of the present day, responsibility as an attribute of character mostly bears the sense of veracity and dependability; a responsible person is one who can be counted on to speak the truth and to keep his word. For such persons the taking of oaths would seem to be superfluous. When the Confession affirms that the taking of oaths is a legitimate religious act for Christians, it does so because it interprets the responsibility of Christians in a different way; it views it in terms of their relation to God rather than in terms of qualities of character. So far as their own characters are concerned, Christians have neither the right to assume an absolute obligation, nor the power to fulfill it, since they are sinful, fallible, and weak, like all others. They can express their responsibility only by committing themselves to the faithfulness of God and submitting themselves to his judgment, in the assurance that though we are faithless, "he abideth faithful." (II Tim. 2:13.) The taking of an oath is an act of such commitment. Obviously it cannot be used as a cover for falsehood and insincerity. In doing it the Christian pledges himself to an absolute obligation, but he does this, not because of a claim to possess in himself the qualities of character that could sustain it, but as an act of faith in the faithfulness of God. This is the meaning of justification by faith, and it determines the character of the Christian life as a whole. It is not because Christians are possessed of superior moral qualities, but because they are committed persons, that they are to be trusted and relied on. And this is the reason why it is stated in Paragraph 4 that an oath is binding, even in circumstances where that might seem neither rational nor expedient; for an oath is more than a human assertion or promise raised to the nth degree.

CF XXIV,5   A vow is of the like nature with a promissory oath, and ought to be made with the like religious care, and to be performed with the like faithfulness.

CF XXIV,6   It is not to be made to any creature, but to God alone: and that it may be accepted, it is to be made voluntarily, out of faith and conscience of duty, in way of thankfulness for mercy received, or for obtaining of what we want; whereby we more strictly bind ourselves to necessary duties, or to other things, so far and so long as they may fitly conduce thereunto.

CF XXIV,7   No man may vow to do anything forbidden in the word of God, or what would hinder any duty therein commanded, or which is not in his own power, and for the performance whereof he hath no promise or ability from God. In which respects, monastical vows of perpetual single life, professed poverty, and regular obedience, are so far from being degrees of higher perfection, that they are superstitious and sinful snares, in which no Christian may entangle himself.

Vows are similar to oaths, except that they are made to God alone, and do not involve third parties. (This strict usage is not consistently followed in the language of the present day; baptismal vows and marriage vows do involve third parties, although it remains true that they are made to God primarily.) They are acts of personal commitment to God. They are not to be construed as measures taken to exact favors from him, or, like vows of celibacy, poverty, and "regular obedience" (i.e., obedience to a monastic rule), to obtain superior merit with him.

▪ chapter XXV[1]

OF THE CIVIL MAGISTRATE

CF XXV,1   God, the Supreme Lord and King of all the world, hath ordained civil magistrates to be under him over the people, for his own glory and the public good; and to this end, hath armed them with the power of the sword, for the defense and encouragement of them that are good, and for the punishment of evildoers.

The two preceding chapters were intended to summarize our duty toward God, which is contained in the first table of the law. (CF XXI, 2.) The Confession now turns to the second table and our duty toward our fellow men, which it treats in this and the following chapter. The Confession limits its attention to the political and marital aspects of Christian responsibility; and, though these are undoubtedly of prime importance, and may have been sufficient for the time at which the Confession was drawn up, they can hardly be considered adequate for the present day. The changed conditions of modern life which have been brought about by the development of industrialization and the consequent transformation of social patterns have substantially modified the context of Christian living; and a statement of Christian responsibility adequate to these conditions would have to unfold it in its social and economic dimensions as well. This will not be easy, for difficult and complex questions are involved. Yet such a statement is urgently required for the guidance of

---

1 Chapter XXIII in the Confession of Faith of the United Presbyterian Church in the USA.

Christians who need to know, for example, what the eighth commandment means in terms of the vast and intricate economic structures of modern society.

The present chapter deals with what is now called the relation of church and state. It is an area in which are found some of the most complex and delicate problems Christians have to face.

The statement presupposes "the separation of church and state," in the sense that they have different functions and powers, but it lays it down that the state, no less than the church, is an institution ordained by God for a purpose which is appointed by his will. That purpose is described here in broad terms as the public good; and this may be compared with the statement of the Declaration of Independence, which defines the function of the state as that of securing the fundamental rights of man, or the Preamble to the Constitution of the United States, which speaks of the promotion of the general welfare. Since the functions of both church and state concern the lives of the same people, it is not always easy to draw a clear line of demarcation between them, and there are areas in which friction is almost bound to arise. But in general terms it may be said that the church is concerned with the ends for which men live, while the state is concerned only with the means; the state, in other words, exists in order to maintain and promote the conditions of order and justice under which men may live in community, but it takes no direct concern with the ultimate ends to which they may then devote their lives. However, since the public good or the general welfare are included in the purpose of God, the officer of the state, or "civil magistrate," who is concerned with them, is a minister of God, as Paul says in Romans 13:4.

In the Middle Ages this doctrine of the state was sometimes taken to mean that the state is, or should be, subordinate to the church, and the papacy was regarded as the repository of all authority, both spiritual and temporal. The doctrine, without this particular corollary, continued to be held in the lands of the Reformation, where both church and state accepted the view that both are divine institutions, parallel to but independent of each other. It is noteworthy that even in the United States of America, where the lines of demarcation between church and state were more firmly drawn than elsewhere, the state has continued to regard itself as discharging its function "under God."

The recognition of the state as a divine institution presents no serious problem to Christians in those cases where the state itself accepts this religious or theological interpretation of itself, especially if, in addition, it accepts the democratic principle that all questions of policy are to be determined on the basis of free discussion by the elected representatives of the people. The position of Christians is different in those states which recognize no limit to their competence and assume the right to exercise total control over their citizens and to prescribe the ends for which they shall live. But they are not thereby released from their responsibility toward the state, though it may have to be expressed in a different way. It should not be forgotten that when Paul wrote Romans 13, on which this doctrine of the state as a divine institution is largely based, the state to which he and his readers were subject was the Roman Empire, which certainly did not understand itself in this way, and which was soon to assume the guise of the beast from the abyss, drunk with the blood of the saints, which is portrayed in Revelation 13. The Confession confines its attention to the position of Christians in a "Christian" state; it does not contemplate the kind of situation in which their responsibility may have to be expressed in the form of protest, resistance, and even rebellion.

CF XXV,2   It is lawful for Christians to accept and execute the office of a magistrate, when called thereunto; in the managing whereof, as they ought especially to maintain piety, justice, and peace, according to the wholesome laws of each commonwealth, so, for that end, they may lawfully, now under the New Testament, wage war upon just and necessary occasions.

This statement is directed against the view which was vigorously championed by some sects at the time of the Reformation, that Christians, by virtue of their allegiance to Christ and his kingdom, are excluded from active participation in the affairs of the kingdoms and states of this world. This view is now held only by small groups, like the Mennonites, who fear that any engagement by Christians in political activity is bound to involve them in compromise with their faith and their absolute obedience to Christ. The view of the majority has always been that, while Christians are not *of* this world, they have nevertheless to be Christians *in* this world (John 17:15), and, since the state is divinely instituted to take care of men's lives in this world, they may properly accept political office and engage in political activity in the fulfillment of their vocation. But this does not dispose of the problem entirely. There are many Christians who, while accepting the general principle of political responsibility, are troubled in conscience over the question whether certain methods of political action are compatible with the vocation of a Christian, especially some which involve the use of force. The civil magistrate, according to Paragraph 1 (which echoes the language of Romans 13:4), is armed with the power of the sword. The reference is primarily to the powers of law enforcement within the jurisdiction of the state, and since these, for the most part, do not involve bloodshed, no serious problem arises here, although there are some persons who oppose the infliction of the death penalty even in cases of murder. When the sword is thought of, however, as a weapon of war, to be used against the citizens of another state with intent to destroy their lives, the problem becomes acute for many Christians who feel that this is a method of political action in which they could not participate without betraying their faith. The Confession affirms that participation in war is lawful upon just and necessary occasions. It is open to question whether the action of Christians is to be regulated only by considerations of justice and necessity; and, apart from that, there is the problem of determining when the occasion is just and necessary. Some contend that war is never necessary, and seldom just; and their position has been strengthened by the changed character of modern war, which has acquired such vast potentialities of destruction as to render it virtually suicidal for all who participate, and perhaps even for the human race. Others hold that with the existence of an international tribunal for the adjudication of disputes, an authoritative judgment on the justice and necessity of war on any specific occasion can now be rendered and may be accepted as such by Christians. There is no easy resolution of the difference between these two views. Both are conscientiously held, and both must be respected. It scarcely needs to be added that, while Christians may differ on the question of participation in war, they must surely be united in striving by every means in their power to avert war on every specific occasion on which it threatens, and to secure the general renunciation of war as an instrument of political action.

CF XXV,3   Civil magistrates may not assume to themselves the administration of the word and sacraments; or the power of the keys of the kingdom of heaven; or, in the least, interfere in matters of faith. Yet, as nursing fathers, it is the duty of civil magistrates to protect the church of our common Lord, without giving the preference to any denomination of Christians above the rest, in such a manner that all ecclesiastical persons whatever shall enjoy the full, free, and unquestioned liberty of discharging every part of their sacred functions, without violence or danger. And, as Jesus Christ hath appointed a regular government and discipline in his church, no law of any commonwealth should interfere with, let, or hinder, the due exercise thereof, among the voluntary members of any denomination of Christians, according to their own profession and belief. It is the duty of civil magistrates to protect the person and good name of all their people, in such an effectual manner as that no person be suffered, either upon pretense of religion or infidelity, to offer any indignity, violence, abuse, or injury to any other person whatsoever: and to take order, that all religious and ecclesiastical assemblies be held without molestation or disturbance.

CF XXV,4   It is the duty of the people to pray for magistrates, to honor their persons, to pay them tribute and other dues, to obey their lawful commands, and to be subject to their authority, for conscience' sake. Infidelity, or difference in religion, doth not make void the magistrate's just and legal authority, nor free the people from their due obedience to him: from which ecclesiastical persons are not exempted; much less hath the Pope any power or jurisdiction over them in their dominions, or over any of their people; and least of all to deprive them of their dominions or lives, if he shall judge them to be heretics, or upon any other pretense whatsoever.

Since church and state are instituted by God and occupy their respective spheres by his appointment, they are bound to recognize each other, to respect each other, and to assist each other by the means and in the measure proper to each. Thus it is the duty of the state to afford the church the common protection of the laws, to recognize the freedom of its members to exercise their faith, and to acknowledge its right to employ its own government and discipline—and all with complete impartiality toward those of all denominations. The reciprocal duty of the church toward the state is to pray for it, to respect its officers, to obey its laws, and to pay its dues. And this duty stands, even though officers of the state be unbelievers or adherents of another faith; they are still to be regarded by Christians as instruments of the authority of God.

Here again, it may be noted, the Confession does not envisage the situation in which a state sets itself in ideological opposition to the church, though this kind of situation may be held to be covered implicitly in the concluding repudiation of papal claims.

■ chapter XXVI[1]

OF MARRIAGE AND DIVORCE

CF XXVI,1   Marriage is a union between one man and one woman, designed of God to last so long as they both shall live.

CF XXVI,2   Marriage is designed for the mutual help of husband and wife; for the safeguarding, undergirding, and development of their moral and spiritual character; for the propagation of children and the rearing of them in the discipline and instruction of the Lord.

The institution of marriage is introduced here, as was suggested in the introductory note to CF XXV, 1, because it is the focal point of the social responsibility of Christians. Man is, by nature, a social being; he is created to live, not by himself alone, but in society with his brother man. Brotherhood, however, derives its meaning from the more ultimate relationship of marriage; brothers are the offspring of an enduring union between one man and one woman. Thus it is that in the creation narrative, marriage is introduced as the divine antidote to an existence in solitude: "And the Lord God said, It is not good that the man should be alone; I will make him an help meet for him." (Gen. 2:18.)

---

[1] This chapter was substituted by the Presbyterian Church in the United States, in 1959, for the original chapter prepared by the Westminster Assembly. Chapter XXIV of the Confession of Faith of the United Presbyterian Church in the USA is also a revision of the original, on similar lines; it was first adopted by the Presbyterian Church in the USA (as it then was) in 1953.

Marriage is the basic social unit and the node of all social relationships.

The real ground of monogamy lies in the marriage relationship itself, which is of such a nature that it can be fully entered into only by one man and one woman at the same time. It involves such a total acceptance of each by the other and such a total commitment of each to the other, that their lives cease to be separate units and become fused in a higher identity; in the language of the Bible, "they shall be one flesh." (Gen. 2:24; the reference is to more than the physical aspect of the relationship.) When the Confession says that marriage is designed for the mutual help of husband and wife, we must not think only of the mutual help, since that would place marriage on much the same level as a business partnership; the important thing is the new personal relationship which is constituted by it. Partners in marriage are more than parties to a contract; they become related to each other in such a way that they cease to be merely a man and a woman, they are now husband and wife.

At the same time the new relationship of husband and wife bears fruit in their personal lives as a man and a woman. As the Confession indicates, marriage provides a shelter, a support, and a school of character. It is a means by which husband and wife may grow to the stature of full manhood and womanhood.

Marriage is also the basis of the family, as the sexual union of husband and wife, by which it is consummated, is the means "for the propagation of children." But the birth of a child to a husband and wife is more than the fulfillment of a biological function. By the birth of a child, husband and wife now become father and mother and assume the responsibility for training their child to become a mature and responsible human being before God.

CF XXVI,3   All persons who are able with judgment to give their consent may marry, except within the limits of blood relationship forbidden by Scripture, and such marriages are valid before God in the eyes of the church. But no marriage can be fully and securely Christian in spirit or in purpose unless both partners are committed to a common Christian faith and to a deeply shared intention of building a Christian home. Evangelical Christians should seek as partners in marriage only persons who hold in common a sound basis of evangelical faith.

In view of the nature of marriage, as it is described in the first two paragraphs, it is obvious that those who enter it must do so of their own free will. Marriage is not a condition that can be imposed on anyone. Yet at the same time marriage cannot be founded on an arbitrary and irresponsible freedom. The Confession points to three considerations by which the freedom to marry should be informed and directed. The first is that those who consent to marry must be "able with judgment" to do so. This ability is usually measured by a person's age; the "legal age" of marriage is the age at which people are deemed to have sufficient judgment to enter marriage without having to obtain the consent of their parents. If marriage is entered upon by people who are lacking in judgment, whether they be of minor age or not, there is the greater risk of its being undertaken on the basis of romantic attachment or sexual attraction, which do not by themselves provide a sufficient basis for a true and enduring marriage, but which have such power in the initial stages that they may blind the persons concerned to incompatibilities between them which darken the prospects of a permanent relationship.

The second limitation on the freedom to marry, to which the Confession refers, has to do with blood relationship between the persons involved. The prohibition of marriage within certain degrees of kinship is based partly on considerations of eugenics (prevention of inbreeding), partly on suspicion of the motivation of such marriages. The definition of these "forbidden degrees" in the law of Leviticus 18, however, cannot be considered binding on Christians, who are not under the law; and in addition, the limits imposed by the Levitical law are not determined by *blood* relationship only. There has been much controversy over the question of marriage with a deceased wife's sister, which was thought to be forbidden in Leviticus 18:18; but it is now recognized that what this law forbids is marriage with two sisters simultaneously in a society in which polygamy is practiced. There is nothing in the law to prohibit marriage with a wife's sister after the wife is dead.

Thirdly, the freedom to marry should be exercised with regard to the religious affinity of the persons concerned. Since marriage is a total union between two persons, a difference of religious faith between them is likely to prove a source of incompatibility and tension; for if one partner is committed to the Christian faith and the other is not, this means that they differ as to the ultimate source, meaning, and goal of life, and a difference between them at so deep a level is bound to have serious effects on their life together and on the quality of the home they build. The further recommendation of the Confession that evangelical Christians should seek their partners in marriage among others of like faith contains an implied warning against what the Roman Catholic Church calls "mixed marriages"; that is, marriages between Roman Catholics and Protestants. The danger in this kind of marriage arises, not so much from differences at the level of ultimate commitment, as rather from the laws of the Roman Catholic Church, which interpose an element of intolerance between the partners to the marriage.

Of course, the "judgment" to be exercised in the choice of partners in marriage is not limited to their religious compatibility. Christians contemplating marriage are advised to explore the question of their compatibility in the most comprehensive way—not that perfect compatibility between two partners in marriage is always possible, or perhaps even desirable; but unless the compatibilities outweigh the incompatibilities, the marriage is threatened with failure. It may be added that a successful marriage also depends on the extent to which those who enter it recognize that marriage is a school, in which the partners must study each other and learn to adjust to each other. Those who consent to marry must also conspire to remain married.

CF XXVI,4   Marriage for the Christian has religious as well as civil significance. The distinctive contribution of the church in performing the marriage ceremony is to affirm the divine institution of marriage; to invoke God's blessing upon those who enter into the marital relationship in accordance with his word; to hear the vows of those who desire to be married; and to assure the married partners of God's grace within their new relationship.

Marriage is both a religious ordinance and a legal contract, and as such it is of concern to both church and state. The state has a legitimate interest in marriage, because the family forms the basic unit in the organization of society, and the stability of the social order is largely dependent on the stability of marriage.[2] It is proper, therefore, that the state should provide a civil ceremony for those who are not committed to the Christian faith and who recognize only the civil significance of marriage. Christians have also to recognize the civil significance of marriage; but since marriage to them is primarily a state of life instituted by God and subject to regulation by his word, it is fitting that this should be expressed in the marriage ceremony provided by the church.

CF XXVI,5   It is the divine intention that persons entering the marriage covenant become inseparably united, thus allowing for no dissolution save that caused by the death of either husband or wife. However, the weaknesses of one or both partners may lead to gross and persistent denial of the marriage vows so that marriage dies at the heart and the union becomes intolerable; yet only

---

[2] Compare this statement from the Order for the Solemnization of Marriage of the Church of Scotland: "It was ordained for the welfare of human society, which can be strong and happy only where the marriage bond is held in honour."

in cases of extreme, unrepented-of, and irremediable unfaithfulness (physical or spiritual) should separation or divorce be considered. Such separation or divorce is accepted as permissible only because of the failure of one or both of the partners, and does not lessen in any way the divine intention for indissoluble union.

Marriage is intended to be a lifelong relationship between husband and wife, and Christians who enter it do so with that intention. It is not a partnership, to be dissolved at any time by consent of parties. It is a vow which they take before God, to take each other "to have and to hold from this day forward; for better, for worse; for richer, for poorer; in sickness and in health, to love and to cherish, till death . . ." Roman Catholics, who regard marriage as a sacrament, hold that the marriage bond is indissoluble; they refuse (in theory) to allow divorce on any grounds. Protestants, while agreeing that the marriage bond is intended to be indissoluble, do not believe that the intention can be legally enforced when the sin or weakness of one or both of the partners has destroyed the marriage from the inside. For the legal contract is only the external and institutional aspect of an internal, personal relationship. It does not create it or sustain it, and it cannot be a substitute for it. It is the shell which encloses the egg. If the egg has gone bad, it will not help matters to preserve the shell unbroken. It is unevangelical to insist on the maintenance of marriage as a matter of law when it has been broken as a matter of fact.

The Confession does not now specify what are valid grounds for separation or divorce (the original chapter allowed only adultery and desertion), but speaks in general terms of "denial of the marriage vows" and "unfaithfulness." Since the dissolution of the marriage contract is a matter for the civil courts, the grounds on which it is allowed are specified in the law of the state. The Confession merely enunciates the principle that the marriage bond should be dissolved only when it is so grievously broken that it cannot be mended.

CF XXVI,6   The remarriage of divorced persons may be sanctioned by the church, in keeping with the redemptive
gospel of Christ, when sufficient penitence for sin and
failure is evident, and a firm purpose of and endeavor
after Christian marriage is manifested.

If the church recognizes, however reluctantly, that divorce is
permissible under certain circumstances, it cannot consistently
refuse to sanction the remarriage of divorced persons. To condemn such persons to remain unmarried would not be "in keeping with the redemptive gospel of Christ," which aims at the
saving of men's lives, not their destruction. Some churches make
a compromise by conceding remarriage to the innocent party in a
divorce and denying it to the guilty; but in order to apply the
distinction they have to rely on the verdict of the civil court,
which, though it may be reliable enough, is hardly a valid norm
for the action of the church. In this matter, as in all others, the
church's action, as the Confession points out, must be regulated
by the gospel; that is, it must have regard to penitence for past sin
and purpose of new obedience—although difficulty may be found
in determining in specific cases whether the penitence manifested
by applicants for remarriage is "sufficient" and the purpose of
amendment "firm."

CF XXVI,7   Divorced persons should give prayerful thought to
discover if God's vocation for them is to remain unmarried, since one failure in this realm raises serious
question as to the rightness and wisdom of undertaking
another union.

Though the divine institution of marriage is open to all, it is
not obligatory upon all. There is no commandment which says,
Thou shalt marry; and there are people for whom the purpose
of their lives is to be fulfilled without marriage. The Confession
suggests here that divorce may be the means by which some
people discover that they belong to this exceptional category,
and it adds the more mundane consideration that those who have

failed in marriage once are not likely to succeed a second time. This cautionary note—which may sound over-cautionary to some —is timely, in view of current practice in some circles of society, where the rule seems to be, If at first you don't succeed, try, try, try . . . again!

■ chapter XXVII[1]

OF THE CHURCH

It is a weakness of the Confession of Faith, which it shares with others of the same tradition, that it does not introduce the church until this comparatively late stage. It could, of course, be argued that the church is presupposed from the beginning, and that is partly true. Yet the fact that the constitution and nature of the Christian life and ethic are treated before the introduction of the church as a specific theme is likely to give the impression (and has in fact done so) that the church is one element in the Christian life, and to obscure the fact that the church is itself the element in which the Christian life is lived. It is significant perhaps, and certainly unfortunate, that in the Shorter Catechism, the most popular of all the Westminster Standards, the church is omitted altogether. There can be no Christian life apart from the church. A Christian outside the church is as impossible as a fish out of the water.

CF XXVII,1   The catholic or universal church, which is invisible, consists of the whole number of the elect, that have been, are, or shall be gathered into one, under Christ the head thereof; and is the spouse, the body, the fullness of him that filleth all in all.

CF XXVII,2   The visible church, which is also catholic or universal under the gospel (not confined to one nation

---

[1] Chapter XXV in the Confession of Faith of the United Presbyterian Church in the USA.

as before under the law), consists of all those throughout the world that profess the true religion, together
with their children; and is the kingdom of the Lord
Jesus Christ; the house and family of God, through
which men are ordinarily saved and union with
which is essential to their best growth and service.

The distinction between the visible and the invisible church
has been the subject of much misunderstanding. It was introduced by the Reformers of the sixteenth century in order to con-
test the claim that the church is simply identical with the institution which is headed by the Bishop of Rome and which is
called the Roman Catholic Church, and that church membership
means only membership in this institution. The claim of Rome
to be the only authentic church of Jesus Christ is generally based
on the arguments that it was founded by him, that it has existed
continuously since its foundation, and that it has been preserved
by the power of the Holy Spirit from error or sin or loss of
identity. In view of the glaring discrepancies which they found
between the actual practice of the church and the authoritative
standard of the New Testament, the Reformers were constrained
to reject the church's claim to inerrancy and infallibility. But they
did not reject the church, nor did they intend to teach, as they
have sometimes been thought to have done, that membership in
the visible church is of little or no importance for Christians. The
distinction between the visible and the invisible church must
not be taken to mean that there are two churches, that true Christians are members of an invisible church, and that, as such, they
need have nothing to do with the visible church, which consists
of those who make a profession of religion (often without the
corresponding reality). That is not what the Reformers meant at
all. To them a Christian was always a member of the visible
church and a man who made a visible profession of religion.
What they wanted to stress is that the visible church, with all its
visible members, is continually subject to the judgment of God;
for it is not exempt from sin and error. But they did not make

this an excuse for abandoning the church. On the contrary, it was this that led them to discover the true secret of the church's life; for the visible life of the church, like that of every Christian, consists in the drawing of continual reformation and renewal from the invisible source of the grace of God. While Roman Catholics hold that the church is essentially "irreformable," the church which calls itself "reformed" recognizes that reformation is the law of its life. The church is visible, and must be visible; but it is visible as the church only when its life makes visible the invisible powers of reformation and renewal that proceed from the word and Spirit of God.

There is, however, one aspect of the distinction drawn in these paragraphs which may be allowed to stand. The visible church refers to the church which exists at the present time and comprises its members who are now living; the invisible church is not limited to its present membership, but comprises all those "that have been, are, or shall be gathered into one, under Christ the head thereof." This feature of our membership in the church, which brings us into union with those who have gone before and those who will come after, as well as those who are members now, is generally treated as an aspect of the communion of saints, which is the theme of the next chapter.

The identification of the church with "the kingdom of the Lord Jesus Christ" lacks a basis in Scripture, which generally speaks of the kingdom of God and only very rarely of a kingdom of Christ. The church must not be identified with the kingdom of God. It is the company of those who receive and respond to the good news of the kingdom (Mark 1:14), who seek the kingdom (Matt. 6:33), who pray for its coming (Matt. 6:10), and to whom the kingdom will be given (Luke 12:32). If it is called the kingdom of Christ, it can only be as the realm in which he is at present accepted as Lord, until the time of the fulfillment of the kingdom of God. (I Cor. 15:24-28.) It should not be taken to mean that the church is vested with any royal prerogatives, save the royal priesthood of intercession. (I Peter 2:9.)

CF XXVII,3   Unto this catholic visible church, Christ hath given
the ministry, oracles, and ordinances of God, for the
gathering and perfecting of the saints, in this life, to
the end of the world: and doth by his own presence
and Spirit, according to his promise, make them effectual thereunto.

The word "catholic" properly means universal, as is indicated
in Paragraphs 1 and 2, and it was originally used in this meaning.
As time went on, it acquired the additional meaning of continuous; and these two elements, universality and continuity, came to
be regarded as marks of the true church. The Reformers rejected
this conception and taught instead that the mark of the true
church is a visible relation to the invisible source of its life. What
is this relation, and how is it manifested? This is the question
which is answered in this paragraph. The Confession says, in
effect, that the marks of the true or catholic church are the possession of certain furnishings and the exercise of certain functions:
"the ministry, oracles, and ordinances of God." The ministry
is not an agency set up by the church but a gift of Christ to the
church. No specific order of ministry is prescribed; this is a matter
to be determined and regulated by the church. The Presbyterian
Church lays the emphasis on the ministerial office or function,
rather than on the order; and when in the act of ordination it
sets men apart for the office of the ministry, it does so with the
intention that they, with their special gifts, may assume this responsibility in behalf of the church as a whole. The oracles and
ordinances refer to the word and the sacraments, which are also
gifts of Christ to the church, and, as their association with the
ministry here indicates, they are primarily instruments or "means
of grace," by which the life that proceeds from Christ the head is
conveyed to the church, his body. A true or catholic church
is one in which the word and the sacraments are used in this
way for the edification or upbuilding of the church.

"for the gathering and perfecting of the saints, in this life."
The ministry of the word and sacraments has as its purpose the

formation of a community of persons who are thereby transformed. Members of the church are not merely spectators or
listeners; still less are they to be thought of as patrons, or parti-
sans, or propagandists: they are saints—that is, participants in
the transforming power of the grace of God.

"to the end of the world." The church is an "eschatological"
community; i.e., it is a community that is on the move toward the
end for which it was called into being. This end consists in the
fulfillment of God's eternal purpose with the world, and, as such,
it transcends the horizons of this world. What this means for the
church and its members will be considered in Chapters XXXII
and XXXIII.

"and doth by his own presence and Spirit, according to his
promise, make them effectual thereunto." The true or catholic
church is the church which recognizes its continual dependence
on the presence and operation of Christ in the Spirit. It cannot
by itself make the word and sacraments effect the purpose for
which they were given. Only he who gave them can do that (CF
I, 5), and the ministry is his instrumentality. That is why prayer
must always have top priority on the agenda of the church. (CF
XXIII, 3-4.)

CF XXVII,4   This catholic church hath been sometimes more,
sometimes less, visible. And particular churches, which
are members thereof, are more or less pure, according
as the doctrine of the gospel is taught and embraced,
ordinances administered, and public worship performed more or less purely in them.

CF XXVII,5   The purest churches under heaven are subject both
to mixture and error: and some have so degenerated
as to become apparently no churches of Christ. Nevertheless, there shall be always a church on earth, to
worship God according to his will.

These paragraphs make it clear that the distinction between
the visible and the invisible church does not point to two different churches but to differences of degree in which the invisible

finds visible expression and embodiment in the church, or any particular church. The standard by which these are measured is the degree of purity with which the equipment and functions listed in Paragraph 3 are employed in the church.

The purpose of this is not so much to provide a basis for the criticism of particular churches, although the Confession states boldly (even more boldly in the original text) that the application of the test might yield negative results in some cases, as rather to affirm the great principle of the Reformation, that the church—every church—stands under the judgment of God and in continual need of reformation; "the purest churches under heaven are subject both to mixture and error." Reformation is the law of the church's life, and it is just for this reason that the Confession affirms the perpetuity of the church; for while the church is never exempt from the need of reformation, it is never so corrupt as to be incapable of it. The church will continue, not because of its own ability to survive, but by the faithfulness of him who builds it and who promised that the gates of death would not prevail against it.

CF XXVII,6   The Lord Jesus Christ is the only head of the church, and the claim of any man to be the vicar of Christ and the head of the church, is without warrant in fact or in Scripture, even anti-Christian, a usurpation dishonoring to the Lord Jesus Christ.

The church is the body of Christ, and he alone is the head of the body. The Confession affirms that the visible expression of the invisible headship of Christ is the absence of any visible head. The Roman Catholic Church, at which this argument is principally aimed, takes the position that the visible headship of the Pope does not conflict with the invisible headship of Christ but constitutes the organ through which it is exercised. The position is plausible in theory. In practice, the presence of a visible head —and especially of one with so much headroom as the Pope—is in danger of obscuring the invisible headship of Christ; and the church (which is subject to error) is better protected against this error when it has no visible head.

■ chapter XXVIII[1]

OF THE COMMUNION OF SAINTS

CF XXVIII,1   All saints being united to Jesus Christ their head,
by his Spirit and by faith, have fellowship with him in
his graces, sufferings, death, resurrection, and glory:
and, being united to one another in love, they have
communion in each other's gifts and graces, and are
obliged to the performance of such duties, public and
private, as do conduce to their mutual good, both in
the inward and outward man.

This chapter deals with the nature of the internal bond by
which members of the church are bound together. This bond is
deeper than membership in the church as an institution. That is
its visible expression. It consists in an invisible relation in which
they stand to Christ, and, thereby, to one another. This relation
is described here in terms of unity, communion, and fellowship,
all of which are equivalent renderings of the great New Testament
word, *koinonia*. This word points to a fundamental feature of
the Christian life, which has often been overlooked. What makes
a man a Christian? Many tend to think of it as something that
takes place in the inward privacy of a man's individual life. According to the New Testament, the really decisive thing that
takes place when a man becomes a Christian is that he is taken
out of his individual privacy and brought into *koinonia,* or fellowship: he is called into the fellowship of Jesus Christ (I Cor.

---

[1] Chapter XXVI in the Confession of Faith of the United Presbyterian
Church in the USA.

1:9) by the fellowship of the Holy Spirit (II Cor. 13:14), and he is thereby brought into fellowship with other Christians (Acts 2:42; I John 1:3), and committed to a life of fellowship (Phil. 2:1-4).

The Christian's relation to Christ is described as "fellowship with him in his graces, sufferings, death, resurrection, and glory." The Christian participates in those acts of Christ in the sense that he accepts them as the basis of his existence. He consents to live— and recognizes that he can only live—as a sinner who is reconciled to God by the grace which he has extended to men in Jesus Christ. He rests his whole existence on Christ, in all its dimensions —his past on the death of Christ, his present on the power of his resurrection, and his future in the hope of his coming in glory.

The fellowship of the Christian with Christ is both the basis and the bond of his fellowship with other Christians. Christians are "united to one another in love"—the same kind of love by which they are united to Christ, not a love based on mutual attraction or affinity or congeniality (for then it would be very restricted in scope), but a love which overcomes divisions and reconciles contraries and brings into communion those who have nothing in common save the fact that Christ gave himself for them.

CF XXVIII,2   Saints by their profession are bound to maintain an holy fellowship and communion in the worship of God, and in performing such other spiritual services as tend to their mutual edification; as also in relieving each other in outward things, according to their several abilities and necessities. Which communion, as God offereth opportunity, is to be extended unto all those who, in every place, call upon the name of the Lord Jesus.

The communion of saints is not only a gift or a privilege which Christians enjoy; it is a task at which they have to work. Because it is theirs, they have to act it out. (Phil. 2:1-4.) They have to practice it in common worship, where their communion with one another is refreshed at its roots in their communion with God, and in mutual support, both spiritual and material. (In the New

Testament the Greek word, *koinonia,* is also used for the collection which the Christians of Greece made for "the poor saints at Jerusalem." See Rom. 15:26; II Cor. 8:4.) And since it is based, not on contiguity, but on their communion with Christ, it must reach out beyond those with whom they are in immediate contact.

CF XXVIII,3   This communion which the saints have with Christ, doth not make them in any wise partakers of the substance of his Godhead, or to be equal with Christ in any respect: either of which to affirm, is impious and blasphemous. Nor doth their communion one with another as saints, take away or infringe the title or property which each man hath in his goods and possessions.

The Confession marks two limitations on the communion of saints. The communion of Christians with Christ has sometimes been spoken of as a mystical union, and it has occasionally been experienced as a rapture or ecstasy in which, like Paul (II Cor. 12:1-2), they have felt they were lifted out of their personal identity and, in some way, fused with the very being of Christ. In some of the religions of the world, especially those of the East, the loss of personal identity through its fusion with the divine is the goal of the mystic quest. The Confession warns against the importation of such notions into Christian piety, which must never transgress the frontiers of personal identity, and especially those which separate man from God. Man's distinctness from God and his responsibility to God are fundamental positions of Christian faith.

The Confession also adds that the communion of saints does not imply communism (in the general sense of communal ownership of property). In view of the experiment of the primitive Christian community in a communist way of living (Acts 2:44-45; 4:32-35), which, though evidently short-lived, has often been repeated by Christian groups (though without notable success), it cannot be said that communism in this sense is inherently incompatible with the Christian ethic. It is a fact that possession of property is a major source of disunity among men. But it does not follow that the abolition of property is necessarily conducive to unity; the possession of property may be an element in that personal responsibility which is a prerequisite of fellowship. Christian fellowship does not depend on the possession or non-possession of property; it embraces both those who have and those who have not in a communion which transcends all distinctions. (Gal. 3:28.)

■ chapter XXIX[1]

OF THE SACRAMENTS

CF XXIX,1   Sacraments are holy signs and seals of the covenant of grace, immediately instituted by God, to represent Christ and his benefits, and to confirm our interest in him: as also to put a visible difference between those that belong unto the church, and the rest of the world; and solemnly to engage them to the service of God in Christ, according to his word.

The sacraments are means of grace, like the word; that is, they are means by which the grace of God in Jesus Christ is communicated to us. They are associated with the word, in which the gospel is verbalized, because the gospel is more than a verbal communication; it is the power of God unto salvation. (Rom. 1:16.) God himself is present and at work in it. It is this more-than-verbal character of the gospel that is expressed in the sacraments. They are symbolical acts in which decisive elements of the gospel are represented dramatically. They are called "signs and seals of the covenant of grace" because by conveying the gospel of grace in another form than words they strengthen our faith. They differ from verbal communication of the gospel also in this respect, that they involve a greater degree of participation by those who receive them. The preaching of the word may be received in an attitude of detachment or indifference; but the sacraments are "applied" (to use the word of the SC, 92) in such

---

[1] Chapter XXVII in the Confession of Faith of the United Presbyterian Church in the USA.

a definite and personal way to those who receive them that the receivers are thereby marked off from others and "engaged" or committed to respond.

CF XXIX,2   There is in every sacrament a spiritual relation, or sacramental union, between the sign and the thing signified; whence it comes to pass that the names and effects of the one are attributed to the other.

CF XXIX,3   The grace which is exhibited in or by the sacraments, rightly used, is not conferred by any power in them; neither doth the efficacy of a sacrament depend upon the piety or intention of him that doth administer it, but upon the work of the Spirit, and the word of institution, which contains, together with a precept authorizing the use thereof, a promise of benefit to worthy receivers.

The apparently tautological statement that the relation or union between the sign and the thing signified in a sacrament is "sacramental" indicates that sacraments are unique, and that their nature and efficacy cannot be determined on the basis of some general theory of symbols. Much of the controversy over the sacraments which has taken place in the Christian church has been over rival *theories*. The position stated by the Confession, which follows that of Calvin, is equivalent to a repudiation of all theories. The use of the sacraments in the church is based, not on some theory as to how they work, but on the fact that they are instituted by Christ, that they are instruments of his Spirit, and that they are accompanied by his promises; and this is why the benefits of a sacrament may in common speech be ascribed to the sign or the thing signified, since in truth it derives from neither—and from both.

CF XXIX,4   There be only two sacraments ordained by Christ our Lord in the gospel, that is to say, baptism and the supper of the Lord: neither of which may be dispensed by any but by a minister of the word, lawfully ordained.

One of the principal points of disagreement between the Roman and Protestant Churches concerns the number of the sacraments. The Roman Church holds seven: baptism, confirmation, penance, orders, the Lord's Supper (or Eucharist), marriage, and extreme unction. The Protestant Churches hold only two, baptism and the Lord's Supper, and reject the rest, partly because of the lack of conclusive evidence that they were instituted by Christ (though all of them have some foothold in the New Testament), and partly because at the time of the Reformation they had become so encrusted with barnacles of corruption and superstition that there seemed to be no alternative to scrapping them altogether. The rule which limits the dispensing of the sacraments to ordained ministers is a matter of church order.

CF XXIX,5   The sacraments of the Old Testament, in regard of the spiritual things thereby signified and exhibited, were, for substance, the same with those of the New.

The Confession has already affirmed the essential unity of God's dealing with his people under the covenant of grace in both the Old Testament and the New. It now relates this specifically to the sacraments. There are obvious resemblances—and obvious differences—between the Old Testament "sacrament" of circumcision and the New Testament sacrament of baptism, as also between the Passover and the Lord's Supper. The Confession regards each as having substantially the same significance and effect.

■ chapter XXX[1]

OF BAPTISM

CF XXX,1   Baptism is a sacrament of the New Testament, ordained by Jesus Christ, not only for the solemn admission of the party baptized into the visible church, but also to be unto him a sign and seal of the covenant of grace, of his ingrafting into Christ, of regeneration, of remission of sins, and of his giving up unto God, through Jesus Christ, to walk in newness of life: which sacrament is, by Christ's own appointment, to be continued in his church until the end of the world.

The general statement about sacraments, which was made at the beginning of the previous chapter, is here specifically related to baptism: it is instituted by Christ, it represents decisive elements of his work and "applies" them to the recipient, who is thereby marked off as one who belongs to Christ and his church and who is committed to the corresponding life. The institution of baptism should not be thought of merely in terms of the express command of Matthew 28:19; just as the institution of the Lord's Supper rests not merely on Christ's command to do this in remembrance of him (I Cor. 11:24), but on his own doing of the thing signified in it. The sacrament of baptism rests ultimately on Christ's own baptism, in which he became "ingrafted" into us, to bring us the benefits of the covenant of grace (Matt. 3:13-15), and which he consummated by his death (Mark 10:38; Luke 12:50).

[1] Chapter XXVIII in the Confession of Faith of the United Presbyterian Church in the USA.

CF XXX,2   The outward element to be used in this sacrament is water, wherewith the party is to be baptized in the name of the Father, and of the Son, and of the Holy Ghost, by a minister of the gospel, lawfully called thereunto.

CF XXX,3   Dipping of the person into the water is not necessary; but baptism is rightly administered by pouring or sprinkling water upon the person.

Baptism, in which a person is dipped into water and emerges again, symbolizes personal renewal. No less than this is extended to men by God in Christ through the Holy Spirit, and he who is baptized in that name dies to his old self and becomes a new man and the bearer of a new name. The symbolism is best seen in total immersion, but since the act is symbolic, this is not necessary.

CF XXX,4   Not only those that do actually profess faith in and obedience unto Christ, but also the infants of one or both believing parents are to be baptized.

The baptism of infants is a matter on which churches are divided. Those who reject infant baptism do so on the ground that the sacrament, by its nature, requires that those who receive it should be able to grasp what it represents and to enter personally into the engagement it involves. They would probably contend that even the definition of the sacrament given in the Confession implies conditions which cannot be literally fulfilled in the case of infants. The fault here, however, may lie, not in the practice of infant baptism, but in the definition of a sacrament, by which it is allegedly disqualified. It should be noted that "sacrament" is not a Biblical word but a term imported into Christian speech as a convenient hold-all for baptism and the Lord's Supper. If it happens to fit the Lord's Supper better than baptism—and this would be likely enough in view of the greater prominence of the Lord's Supper in the life and thought of the church—this may point to a weakness in the definition. In any case, the practice of infant baptism must be considered on its own merits and not subjected to some artificially constructed definition of a sacrament.

Those who defend infant baptism do so on the grounds that the individual is not the exclusive unit of God's dealings with men in the covenant of grace, and that, although infants are incapable of making their individual response, responsibility may properly be assumed for them by their parents. It is accepted that parents have to assume many kinds of responsibilities for their children within the family, and it is hard to see why this should not apply (in even greater measure) within the communion of saints. Moreover, the withholding of baptism from infants would seem to imply that the gospel cannot be extended to us until we are actually capable of responding to it. But this is to impose a limitation upon God, which parents would refuse to accept in their own relation to their children; for they do not withhold their love from their children, or refrain from displaying it, until the children reach an age at which they can reciprocate.

CF XXX,5   Although it be a great sin to contemn or neglect this ordinance, yet grace and salvation are not so inseparably annexed unto it as that no person can be regenerated or saved without it, or that all that are baptized are undoubtedly regenerated.

The governing consideration here is that baptism is a means of grace; it is not a law or a mechanical device. Since baptism has been graciously provided, it is appropriate to seek it and gratefully to accept its benefits. But it would be inappropriate to insist on baptism as an indispensable condition of salvation or to regard it as a device which produces its effect mechanically.

CF XXX,6   The efficacy of baptism is not tied to that moment of time wherein it is administered; yet, notwithstanding, by the right use of this ordinance the grace promised is not only offered, but really exhibited and

> conferred by the Holy Ghost, to such (whether of age or infants) as that grace belongeth unto, according to the counsel of God's own will, in his appointed time.

This statement is intended to meet the problem presented mainly by the baptism of infants who are not capable of apprehending and responding to the sacrament at the time it is administered to them. Inasmuch as the sacrament of baptism represents the gracious action of God, it cannot fail of its effect; but that effect is not necessarily immediate.

CF XXX,7   The sacrament of baptism is but once to be administered to any person.

The reason why the sign of baptism is given only once is the decisive, once-for-all character of the thing signified. The covenant of grace stands on the faithfulness of God. This does not mean that a baptized person cannot become unfaithful to the covenant and fail to fulfill his engagement; but, should such a person become penitent and seek to be restored, it is by the selfsame grace first sealed upon him in his baptism, which, therefore, need not be repeated. Even the Roman Church accepts baptism by those whom it regards as heretics, if it has been correctly performed in the name of the triune God. (Compare Par. 2.)

■ chapter XXXI[1]

OF THE LORD'S SUPPER

CF XXXI,1   Our Lord Jesus, in the night wherein he was betrayed, instituted the sacrament of his body and blood, called the Lord's Supper, to be observed in his church unto the end of the world; for the perpetual remembrance of the sacrifice of himself in his death, the sealing all benefits thereof unto true believers, their spiritual nourishment and growth in him, their further engagement in and to all duties which they owe unto him; and to be a bond and pledge of their communion with him, and with each other, as members of his mystical body.

This paragraph shows how the Lord's Supper, like baptism, conforms to the general definition of a sacrament given in CF XXIX, 1. The main differences between the Lord's Supper and baptism stem from the fact that they belong to different stages of the Christian life. Baptism is the sacrament of initiation by which the individual is introduced to the life in Christ and the communion of saints, and, as such, it is administered only once. The Lord's Supper is the sacrament of nourishment and growth, in which the members of the church participate together, and by which their life of communion with Christ and with one another is continually renewed; it is the sacrament of the Christian community, and it is frequently repeated.

---

[1] Chapter XXIX in the Confession of Faith of the United Presbyterian Church in the USA.

CF XXXI,2   In this sacrament Christ is not offered up to his Father, nor any real sacrifice made at all for remission of sins of the quick or dead, but a commemoration of that one offering up of himself, by himself, upon the cross, once for all, and a spiritual oblation of all possible praise unto God for the same; so that the so-called sacrifice of the mass is most contradictory to Christ's one sacrifice, the only propitiation for all the sins of the elect.

CF XXXI,4   Private masses, or receiving this sacrament by a priest, or any other, alone; as likewise the denial of the cup to the people; worshipping the elements, the lifting them up, or carrying them about for adoration, and the reserving them for any pretended religious use, are all contrary to the nature of this sacrament, and to the institution of Christ.

CF XXXI,6   That doctrine which maintains a change of the substance of bread and wine, into the substance of Christ's body and blood (commonly called transubstantiation) by consecration of a priest, or by any other way, is repugnant, not to Scripture alone, but even to common sense and reason; overthroweth the nature of the sacrament; and hath been, and is, the cause of manifold superstitions, yea, of gross idolatries.

These three paragraphs may be conveniently taken together, out of their numerical order, because they are all directed against the theory and practice of the Roman Catholic Church with regard to the sacrament. According to the theory which was worked out and officially adopted in the Middle Ages, the sacramental bread and wine are, when the priest pronounces the words of consecration, "transubstantiated" (i.e., changed in their substance, although their appearance and other properties remain unchanged) into the body and blood of Christ, and in the mass they are offered again by the priest to the Father, as they were once by

Christ himself on Calvary, as a sacrifice for the sins of the living and the dead. The practice corresponds to the theory; when the bread and wine are believed to be changed into the body and blood of Christ in this way, they are regarded as sacred objects and treated with adoration such as might be given to Christ himself; and to reduce the risk of spilling a drop of the blood of Christ, the cup, which is thought to contain it, is handled only by the priest and withheld from the people.

The Confession rejects the theory of transubstantiation on a number of counts: it has no basis in Scripture; it is contrary to reason, for a thing cannot change in substance and retain all its outward properties unchanged; it "overthroweth the nature of the sacrament," for if the sign is changed into the thing signified, it is no longer a sign of it; and the practices to which it gives rise are superstitious and idolatrous, since they consist in paying divine honors to, and expecting divine blessings from, created things. The Confession also rejects the notion of the sacrament as a re-offering of the sacrifice of Christ; for the sacrifice he offered once on Calvary is itself final and needs no repetition. The sufficiency and once-for-all-ness of what Christ has done for us is the foundation of evangelical faith. The Lord's Supper commemorates and represents the sacrifice of Christ, and the only sacrifice it involves on our part is the "spiritual oblation" of praise and thanksgiving. (See Heb. 13:15.)

CF XXXI,3   The Lord Jesus hath, in this ordinance, appointed his ministers to declare his word of institution to the people, to pray, and bless the elements of bread and wine, and thereby to set them apart from a common to an holy use; and to take and break the bread, to take the cup, and (they communicating also themselves) to give both to the communicants; but to none who are not then present in the congregation.

CF XXXI,5   The outward elements in this sacrament, duly set apart to the uses ordained by Christ, have such relation to him crucified, as that truly, yet sacramentally only, they are sometimes called by the name of the things they represent, to wit, the body and blood of Christ; albeit, in substance and nature, they still remain truly, and only, bread and wine, as they were before.

CF XXXI,7 Worthy receivers, outwardly partaking of the visible elements in this sacrament, do then also inwardly by faith, really and indeed, yet not carnally and corporally, but spiritually, receive and feed upon Christ crucified, and all benefits of his death: the body and blood of Christ being then not corporally or carnally in, with, or under the bread and wine; yet as really, but spiritually, present to the faith of believers in that ordinance, as the elements themselves are to their outward senses.

These paragraphs set forth the main essentials of the doctrine held in the Reformed and Presbyterian Churches. The bread and wine are not changed into the body and blood of Christ, but when they are used according to Christ's appointment, with prayer and thanksgiving, to represent his body and blood, they become means by which those who so receive them have real communion with Christ in his death. The body and blood of Christ are present to the faith of believers as really as the bread and wine are present to their senses; but this reality is "spiritual," i.e., it is the work of the Holy Spirit; it does not depend on any theory, neither transubstantiation, nor consubstantiation, the Lutheran variant of it, according to which the body and blood of Christ are "in, with, and under" the bread and the wine.

Since the Lord's Supper is the sacrament of communion, the Confession restricts participation to those actually present in the congregation. (Par. 3.) This was intended primarily as a means of preventing the abuses denounced in Paragraph 4, and it is sound in principle. But to insist on physical presence in one place seems to be unduly rigid and to inflict hardship on those who for sickness or other reasons are unable to be present; surely they are not to be excluded on that account from the communion of saints or the sacrament which belongs to it. If they cannot be present in the congregation, then, if the communion of saints means what it is said to mean in CF XXVIII, 2, it is up to the congregation, through its representatives, to be present with them.

CF XXXI,8   Although ignorant and wicked men receive the outward elements in this sacrament, yet they receive not the thing signified thereby; but by their unworthy coming thereunto are guilty of the body and blood of the Lord, and bring judgment on themselves.

The right use of the sacrament requires an appropriate disposition on the part of those who receive it. They must be "worthy." Their worthiness, however, is not to be measured by moral standards, but by their grasp of what is extended to them in the sacrament and of their own need of it. Conversely, the unworthiness which excludes some men from the real benefit of the sacrament, though they may receive the elements, consists in their imperviousness to the gift offered and to their own condition. Those who do not come seeking life from the body and blood of Christ become guilty of his death.

■ chapter XXXII[1]

OF CHURCH CENSURES

CF XXXII, 1   The Lord Jesus, as king and head of his church, hath therein appointed a government in the hand of church officers, distinct from the civil magistrate.

The subject of this chapter is much broader than the title suggests; it is the authority and functions of church government as a whole. The choice of title is unfortunate, since it directs attention to only one of the functions of church government, and a somewhat negative one at that.

The statement that the church is entitled to have a government of its own has been already made in CF XXV, 3, which deals with the relation between the civil authorities and the church. Since the subject of church government is not developed in the chapter on the church (CF XXVII), as might have been expected, but is reserved for separate treatment in this chapter, this may be taken as an indication of two things: (1) that its government is not a primary or essential aspect of the church, and (2), more specifically, that government is something distinct from ministry. The "church officers," who are entrusted with it, are different from ministers, although they may include ministers; in the Presbyterian form of government the responsibility is shared equally by ministers and elders.

"distinct from the civil magistrate." This is directed against the position, which had some defenders in the Westminster

---

1 Chapter XXX in the Confession of Faith of the United Presbyterian Church in the USA.

Assembly, that the government of the church should be identical with, or subordinate to, the civil government. This position (which is known as Erastianism) obtains, more or less, in the case of established churches. The complete distinction of the government of the church from that of the state, which the Confession demands, is essential to the independence and integrity of the church.

CF XXXII,2   To these officers the keys of the kingdom of heaven are committed, by virtue whereof they have power respectively to retain and remit sins, to shut that kingdom against the impenitent, both by the word and censures; and to open it unto penitent sinners, by the ministry of the gospel, and by absolution from censures, as occasion shall require.

The principal function assigned to the officers of the church is that of operating the keys of the kingdom of heaven. The Confession adopts here the traditional interpretation of "the power of the keys," associated with the papacy (which claims exclusive possession of it, and represents it on its coat of arms), as the power to grant or withhold absolution from sin and thus to admit persons to heaven or exclude them from it. Careful study of the Biblical passages, on which it is based, reveals that this interpretation, natural enough as it seems, is open to serious question, on two counts. (1) The idea that the power of the keys consists in power to remit or retain sins and so to open or close the gates of heaven can only be obtained by combining Matthew 16:19 with John 20:23. But the assumption that the two passages refer to the same thing is not warranted by the evidence; for the latter makes no reference to the power of the keys or to opening and closing the gates of heaven, and in the former there is no mention of retaining and remitting sins. (2) The more serious objection to the traditional interpretation arises from the peculiar language of Matthew 16:19, which speaks of binding and loosing, and not, as we should expect, of opening and closing. This mode of speech comes from the usage of the Jewish rabbis, who employed these terms to distinguish between interpretations of the law which were considered binding and others which were not. Further comparison of Matthew 23:13 and Luke 11:52 makes it clear that the figure of the keys was used in the same context; what the keys are intended to open is not the gates of heaven, but the gates of knowledge. The power of the keys refers, therefore, not to the power to determine the ultimate destinies of men (for that power belongs to God alone, CF XXXV), but to the awful responsibility laid upon Peter and the apostles of being entrusted with the administration of God's saving will for men.

This responsibility includes "the ministry of the gospel," as the Confession indicates, but, in addition to that, it involves measures for the Christian nurture and support of those who have received the gospel. "Discipline" was the name given by the Reformers to this aspect of the church's responsibility for its members, and it included all appropriate measures for the preservation and promotion of their Christian discipleship. The preoccupation with censures in this chapter reflects the tendency, which early asserted itself in the Reformed Churches, to interpret discipline too exclusively in terms of punishment, and to lose sight of its positive meaning as training. It is an unfortunate consequence of this that church discipline is still thought of as having to do with procedures followed in dealing with offenders. And if discipline has become inoperative to a large extent in the church at the present time, this is probably due to the neglect of its more positive aspect; for it is meaningless and futile for the church to apply "censures" to its members, if it is not at the same time taking positive measures to nurture them in living the Christian life—just as it would be meaningless and futile for parents to punish their children while doing nothing to train them.

Happily, the emphasis in the contemporary church has shifted to the more positive aspects of its care of its members, and discipline is now approached, less in the mood of the law court, and more in that of the family, the school, the hospital. The more discipline in the positive sense becomes a reality in the life of the church, the greater will be the possibility of its application in the other.

CF XXXII,3   Church censures are necessary for the reclaiming and gaining of offending brethren; for deterring of others from like offenses; for purging out of that leaven which might infect the whole lump; for vindicating the honor of Christ, and the holy profession of the gospel; and for preventing the wrath of God, which might justly fall upon the church, if they should suffer his covenant, and the seals thereof, to be profaned by notorious and obstinate offenders.

The main purposes of church discipline are presented here in a somewhat broader perspective and with a clearer view of its positive side than in Paragraph 2. But while "the reclaiming and gaining of offending brethren" is put first, it remains true that the church's responsibility for the care of its erring members may, in the context of its overarching responsibility to Christ, have to take the form of cutting them off. Those against whom extreme measures have to be taken are described as "notorious and obstinate offenders." If obstinacy means persistence in the offense and refusal to repent of it, the case would seem to be clear, but to measure the gravity of an offense by its notoriety is surely to throw the door open to Pharisaism and hypocrisy.

CF XXXII,4   For the better attaining of these ends, the officers of the church are to proceed by admonition, suspension from the sacrament of the Lord's Supper for a season, and by excommunication from the church, according to the nature of the crime, and demerit of the person.

Of the three methods to be employed in church discipline, "admonition," the first named, translates a Greek word in the New Testament which has a more positive connotation than the English term (it is translated "instruction" in Ephesians 6:4, RSV). The difference between the other two is the difference between temporary and permanent exclusion from the membership of the church. The Confession does not specify the gravity of the offense which calls for the extreme measure of excommunication; but it appears to suggest that the matter is to be determined by judicial criteria, and it takes no account of the penitence or impenitence of the offender, which are referred to in Paragraph 2. Excommunication is rarely resorted to in the Presbyterian Churches today, and it would not be regarded as final.

◾ chapter XXXIII[1]

OF SYNODS AND COUNCILS

CF XXXIII,1   For the better government and further edification of the church, there ought to be such assemblies as are commonly called synods or councils: and it belongeth to the overseers and other rulers of the particular churches, by virtue of their office, and the power which Christ hath given them for edification, and not for destruction, to appoint such assemblies; and to convene together in them, as often as they shall judge it expedient for the good of the church.

The subject of church government was introduced in the previous chapter with reference to the "particular church," or local congregation, which carries the immediate responsibility for the care and discipline of its members. But the local congregation is not the church; it is the local branch of the church, and it can no more stand by itself than the local post office can stand apart from its communications with the post office in all other parts of the country and the world. Thus the "church officers," who are charged primarily with the government of the local congregation, have also a concern with the government of the church as a whole; and so the Confession recommends that "for the *better* government and *further* edification of the church" the officers of the local congregation ought to meet from time to time with the officers of other congregations to take counsel together

---

1 Chapter XXXI in the Confession of Faith of the United Presbyterian Church in the USA.

on matters which are of common concern to them. It should be noted that the recommendation is for periodic assemblies or comings-together (this is the literal meaning of "synods"), and not for a permanent organization. The latter is not necessarily excluded; but the existence of a supra-congregational organization (and officers) does tend to move the church's center of gravity from the place where it properly belongs—in the life of the congregation. This is the danger against which the congregational churches took their historic position, although it is to be feared that even they have not escaped the prevailing trend toward bureaucratization.

CF XXXIII,2   It belongeth to synods and councils, ministerially, to determine controversies of faith, and cases of conscience; to set down rules and directions for the better ordering of the public worship of God, and government of his church; to receive complaints in cases of mal-administration, and authoritatively to determine the same: which decrees and determinations, if consonant to the word of God, are to be received with reverence and submission, not only for their agreement with the word, but also for the power whereby they are made, as being an ordinance of God, appointed thereunto in his word.

The functions of synods and councils concern the determination of questions of faith and ethics and the ordering of worship and government, which affect the church as a whole, and with which the local congregation is clearly incompetent to deal. The Confession appears to use synods and councils as synonymous terms, but in view of the distinction indicated in the following paragraph between those which are "general" (that is, those which are representative of the whole Christian church, and for which "councils" would be deemed the appropriate name) and those which are "particular" (that is, those which are representative of some geographical area or of what is now called a denomination), some distinction between their respective spheres of competence would seem to be called for. The view is held by some, for example, that there are matters of faith which could only be properly determined by a general or ecumenical council.

Synods and councils have also to serve as courts of appeal from the decisions of inferior (congregational) courts. And while their own decisions cannot overrule the word of God, they do overrule the decisions of inferior courts, since their superior authority is founded on the word of God. In other words, the Confession holds that a graded hierarchy of church courts is sanctioned by Scripture.

CF XXXIII,3 All synods or councils since the apostles' times, whether general or particular, may err, and many have erred; therefore they are not to be made the rule of faith or practice, but to be used as a help in both.

Since every church court, whatever degree of authority it possesses, is subject to the supreme authority of the word of God, which is the only infallible rule of faith and practice, none can claim to be itself infallible. The statement is aimed principally at the claim of the Roman Catholic Church to possess within itself (though its precise location was long in dispute) an infallible organ. The Confession rejects this claim, not only on the general ground that all church courts, being composed of human beings, are subject to error, but on the more specific historical observation that decisions rendered by such allegedly infallible organs are in fact not "consonant to the word of God" (for example, the Roman dogmas concerning the Virgin Mary—her immaculate conception and bodily assumption). But this does not mean that the decisions of synods and councils (which form a main element in what is commonly called the tradition of the church) are of no value; they can provide valuable help and guidance in the interpretation of the word (as the Westminster Confession of Faith, itself the product of an ecclesiastical synod, is, presumably, now doing), so long as it is remembered that their authority is always subject to the superior authority of the word of God.

CF XXXIII,4   Synods and councils are to handle or conclude nothing but that which is ecclesiastical: and are not to intermeddle with civil affairs which concern the commonwealth unless by way of humble petition in cases extraordinary; or by way of advice for satisfaction of conscience, if they be thereunto required by the civil magistrate.

While the authorities of the church, like those of the state (CF XXV, 3), are normally to confine their activities to their own proper domains and not to confuse the things which belong to Caesar with those which belong to God, there are areas in which their concerns overlap. Some matters of a political nature involve questions of principle or conscience, and on these the church is entitled to make known its position; it may act on its own initiative, if it regards the matter as sufficiently urgent, or it may act at the request of the civil authority (an unlikely contingency today). It may sometimes be difficult to determine when such exceptional cases arise, but these do not affect the fundamental position stated here, which is the right of the church to express its mind on questions that arise in a political context, if they involve moral and spiritual issues.

■ chapter XXXIV[1]

OF THE STATE OF MAN AFTER DEATH,
AND OF THE RESURRECTION OF THE DEAD

The last two chapters of the Confession deal with what is now commonly called eschatology, or the doctrine of the last things (*eschata* being the Greek word for "last things"). A better name for it would be the doctrine of the Christian hope; for this name, besides being Biblical, would bring out more clearly how this doctrine affects our existence in the present (since we cannot live in the present without hope), and it would also remind us of the limitations that are imposed on all attempts to define and spell out the last things (since the Christian hope exceeds the limits, not only of the definable, but also of the conceivable, Romans 8:24; I Corinthians 2:9).

Christian hope is not founded on specific predictions or previews of things to come, which are to be found in the Bible (and which may be arranged by different interpreters in a kaleidoscopic variety of patterns); it is founded on faith in Christ. It might be called the future-pointing dimension of faith in Christ. Its basis is the whole fact of Christ, and especially his resurrection, in which he broke through the barrier which bounds all our future prospects, and opened up a new future. Christian hope is inseparably bound up with Christian faith; it looks forward to the future consummation of what Christ has done for us in the past and the present, when he comes again in the kingdom of his

---

[1] Chapter XXXII in the Confession of Faith of the United Presbyterian Church in the USA.

Father. (CF VIII, 4-5.) Christian hope is not really directed to "things to come," but to "Him who is to come"; and, having that assurance, it does not demand a detailed specification of the things that will happen at his coming.

CF XXXIV,1   The bodies of men, after death, return to dust, and see corruption; but their souls (which neither die nor sleep), having an immortal subsistence, immediately return to God who gave them. The souls of the righteous, being then made perfect in holiness, are received into the highest heavens, where they behold the face of God in light and glory, waiting for the full redemption of their bodies; and the souls of the wicked are cast into hell, where they remain in torments and utter darkness, reserved to the judgment of the great day. Besides these two places for souls separated from their bodies, the Scripture acknowledgeth none.

The distinctive feature of the Christian hope is that it does not come to a halt at the limit of death but looks to a fulfillment "after death." A hope so daring in its range must, it is obvious, have a firm foundation on which to rest, if it is not to be dismissed as a piece of wishful thinking. But the danger of wishful thinking is especially great here, in view of the natural and understandable reluctance of men to accept the grim fact of death at its face value. The inexorable finality with which death closes off all earthly prospects and severs all earthly ties has prompted men to seek some way to prove to themselves that death is not the absolute end and to discover some prospect of a continuance after death. One of these, which is of great antiquity and which is endorsed by the Confession, is the theory of the immortality of the soul; according to this theory it is only the body that dies, the soul does not die; indeed, the soul is incapable of dying, "having an immortal subsistence"—this argument is derived from Plato, who reasoned that since only things that are composed of parts can fall to pieces, the soul, being a simple and uncompounded essence, as he thought, cannot be dissolved. The idea of the immortality of the soul was received in the Christian church very early, and there it was combined with the idea of the resurrection of the body (in a manner which would have horrified Plato, who despised the body). This combination, which was long accepted as orthodox, can be defended on a number of grounds: (1) In several passages the Bible appears to imply the continued existence of the soul after the dissolution of the body (e.g., Ps. 49:15; Matt. 10:28). (2) The view, expressed in the Confession, that death consists in the separation of the soul from the body, receives some plausibility from the observed fact that at death the body remains (for a time), while it is obvious that something has departed from it. (3) If death means the extinction of the whole man, and the life of the resurrection is wholly discontinuous with this life, it is difficult to account for the continuing identity of the individual; the immortality of the soul provides a basis for this.

On the other hand, however, there are several reasons which have led many people to question whether the immortality of the soul should be considered an integral part of the Christian hope: (1) Though the Bible envisages the survival of the soul after death, it gives no support to the idea that the soul is immortal, i.e., incapable of dying; such a thought would tend to blur the distinction, so important in the Bible, between man, who has his "appointed time" (Job 7:1), and God, "who only hath immortality" (I Tim. 6:16). (3) If death means the separation of an immortal soul from a mortal body, and if the soul is the bearer of the self, man cannot really be said to die at all; he merely "shuffles off this mortal coil." This hardly seems to accord with the Biblical attitude toward death, which is presented not only as an inescapable fact which must be taken with full seriousness as the appointed end of all men (Heb. 9:27), but as a fact which has acquired a double seriousness for man who is a sinner—"the sting of death is sin" (I Cor. 15:56). From the Biblical point of view the theory of the immortality of the soul looks like a sophisticated attempt to take the sting out of death. (4) The idea of the immortality of the soul is too fragile and precarious a foundation to support the hope of the life to come. The Christian hope is based, not on human prospects for survival, but on the promises of God, which are more sure.

"waiting for the full redemption of their bodies." One reason why Christian thought has been hospitable to the idea of the immortality of the soul is that it was found helpful in providing a solution to the problem of "the intermediate state"; that is, the state of the individual in the interval between the end of his own life and the end of the world. The focus of the Christian hope in the New Testament is on the end of the world; the coming of Christ, the resurrection of the dead, the last judgment, and the final disposition of mankind all belong here. Does the individual come into the enjoyment of this hope immediately at his own death, or does he have to wait for the end of the world? The Confession answers that the soul passes to its final and eternal destiny immediately after death, while the body awaits the end of the world; the soul has only to wait for its reunion with the body.

The obvious objection to this ingenious theory is that, if the souls of the righteous and the souls of the wicked are assigned to their appointed places immediately after death, there would seem to be no meaning left to the last judgment (which is the theme of the next chapter); for if the sentences are already executed on the souls, what need is there for them to be pronounced on the souls-reunited-with-their-bodies? Another difficulty arises from the implied conception of the relation between time and eternity. How alike are they, and how different? These are extremely complex and difficult questions. The Confession appears to regard time and eternity as two forms of existence which run parallel to each other and which are fundamentally similar in kind, so that, while the soul passes at death from the temporal to the eternal order, it is nevertheless said to *wait* for its reunion with the body, which remains in the temporal order and is there subject to dissolution and decay. This conception is rather artificial, and it implies a degree of knowledge of conditions beyond the limits of the temporal order, to which we, whose experience lies wholly within that order, cannot pretend.

The final clause of the paragraph is directed against the Roman Catholic doctrine which holds that, in addition to heaven and hell, there are three more "receptacles" for the souls of the departed, the *limbus infantium* for unbaptized infants, the *limbus patrum* for the saints of the Old Testament, and purgatory as a place of further purification for those who, though they died in the grace of God, are not sufficiently pure to be admitted to his presence immediately. These conceptions deserve to be repudiated, not merely because they lack a basis in Scripture (a lack they share with some of the notions advanced by the Confession), but because they detract from the finality of death and the decisiveness and sufficiency of the work of Christ.

CF XXXIV,2   At the last day, such as are found alive shall not die, but be changed: and all the dead shall be raised up with the self-same bodies, and none other, although with different qualities, which shall be united again to their souls for ever.

CF XXXIV,3   The bodies of the unjust shall, by the power of Christ, be raised to dishonor; the bodies of the just, by his Spirit, unto honor, and be made conformable to his own glorious body.

The Confession expresses here two important aspects of the Christian hope: (1) The Christian hope does not look for a mere continuation of the present form of existence. The life of the world to come is of a different order from the life of this world, and in passing from this side to that we must "be changed." (2) Despite whatever change may be involved, we shall retain our identity, and with it our responsibility for what we have done in our life in this world. This is the real point of the emphasis on the resurrection of the body. It is not to assert that the life of the world to come will be physical in character (though there is no reason why it should not be, except an un-Christian prejudice against the body, since the body is among the things God created and called very good). Since a man's personal identity is tied up with his body (he is some-*body*), the preservation of his identity would seem to require some continuation of his body, whatever degree of modification it may have to undergo. With regard to the latter, the notion presented in the Confession that the bodies of those raised up at the last day will be "the self-same bodies, and none other, although with different qualities," is simply an inversion of the kind of change supposed in the Roman dogma of transubstantiation, according to which the bread and wine of the sacrament are changed into something other than bread and wine, though all their qualities remain unchanged. It is not easy to understand how a thing can remain the same while changing its qualities, any more than how it can be changed into something else without changing its qualities. The change is defined concretely, in the case of the bodies of the righteous, as assimilation to the glorified body of Christ; the dishonor, for which the bodies of the wicked are resurrected, is left undefined.

OF THE LAST JUDGMENT

CF XXXV,1   God hath appointed a day, wherein he will judge
the world in righteousness by Jesus Christ, to whom all
power and judgment is given of the Father. In which
day, not only the apostate angels shall be judged; but
likewise all persons, that have lived upon earth, shall
appear before the tribunal of Christ, to give an account
of their thoughts, words, and deeds; and to receive
according to what they have done in the body, whether
good or evil.

In its treatment of the last judgment the Confession faithfully
reflects the manner in which the thought of Christendom has
been affected by the imagery in which this aspect of the gospel is
presented in the New Testament, and especially by the picture
of "the great assize" in the 25th chapter of Matthew, in which
the whole of mankind is gathered at one time in one vast court-
room, as it were, to hear sentence pronounced upon them by the
Judge. While the spatial imagery has not been pressed too literally (it is obviously difficult to conceive of all the generations of
men assembled in one place), the Christian imagination has clung
tenaciously to the temporal, and has thought chiefly of the last
judgment as the judgment which will take place on the last day.
It will be noted that each of the three paragraphs in this chapter
of the Confession begins with a reference to the day. Since this

---

[1] Chapter XXXIII in the Confession of Faith of the United Presbyterian
Church in the USA.

day is known only to God, the emphasis has tended to be laid on
the unpredictable occurrence of the judgment and on the importance of not being caught unprepared. But what gives the
last judgment its awful seriousness is not just that it will take
place on the last (unpredictable) day; it is the fact that it is the
last judgment, the judgment which is final and conclusive and
from which there is no appeal. And if it is the judgment of the
last day, this should not be taken to mean that no judgment
takes place before the last day. According to words of Jesus,
given in the Gospel of John, judgment is going on now; men
are being judged all the time by their response to the light which
came into the world with Jesus Christ. (John 3:17-19.) The significance of the last day is that the judgment which has been
going on in secret will be finally and incontrovertibly brought
to light; it is "the day when God shall judge the secrets of men
by Jesus Christ" (Rom. 2:16), who "will bring to light the hidden
things of darkness, and will make manifest the counsels of the
hearts" (I Cor. 4:5). The last day should not be thought of as the
day on which judgment *begins;* it is the day on which it *ends.*

"he will judge the world in righteousness by Jesus Christ."
This does not mean merely that Jesus Christ will be the agent
of God in this matter, but that he will be, as he is already, the
standard of the judgment. The life of the world will be judged,
not by some impossible divine standard, but by One who himself
participated in it and knows what it is, from the inside.

"the apostate angels." This reference to the more-than-human
dimension of evil is a reminder of the fact that the scope of God's
eternal purpose embraces his whole creation.

"to give an account of their thoughts, words, and deeds; and
to receive according to what they have done." The question has
often been asked: If we are finally to be judged by our works,
what becomes of the great evangelical doctrine of justification by
faith? Reference should be made to the discussion of the relation
between faith and works in Chapters XIII, XV, and XVIII. Here
it may be sufficient to say that while we cannot be justified by our
works, in the sense that we cannot vindicate ourselves by our

works before the judgment of God, it is by our works that we show the reality of our faith in the saving grace of God. And it may be added that the apparent inconsistency is more marked in the writings of Paul, from which the language of the Confession is derived, than in the Gospel of John, where the decisive role of faith in the judgment is made more explicit. (John 3:18, 21.)

CF XXXV,2   The end of God's appointing this day, is for the manifestation of the glory of his mercy in the eternal salvation of the elect; and of his justice in the damnation of the reprobate, who are wicked and disobedient. For then shall the righteous go into everlasting life, and receive that fullness of joy and refreshing which shall come from the presence of the Lord: but the wicked, who know not God, and obey not the gospel of Jesus Christ, shall be cast into eternal torments, and punished with everlasting destruction from the presence of the Lord, and from the glory of his power.

The last judgment points to the vindication of God's eternal purpose through the final and decisive discrimination between all that accords with it and all that opposes it. The good which God has willed and the evil which is contrary to his will (both of which are inextricably mixed up together in this world) will be definitively separated and each will be manifested in its true character. Does this involve a separation within mankind between some who will share in the fulfillment of God's purpose and others who will be permanently excluded from it? The Confession takes this position, and there is undoubtedly a prominent strain in the language of Scripture which supports it. There are some, however, who feel that this position is inconsistent with the gospel of grace and who hold that if some of his children were to be permanently excluded, this would signify the defeat, or partial defeat, of God's purpose of salvation; they point to that other strain in the New Testament which speaks of that purpose as extending to all men (I Tim. 2:4) and of the judgment it entails, not as a separation of mankind into two opposite groups, but as the triumph of God's grace over the sin which opposes it in all mankind: "for God hath concluded them all in unbelief, that he might have mercy upon all" (Rom. 11:32). Both positions can be defended—and attacked—from the perspective of the central New Testament message of the grace of God; for if salvation is by free grace alone, it is equally impossible to affirm that God *must* save all men, as to deny that he *may*. The true position would seem to be that, since the last judgment is God's judgment, no one is competent to make confident assertions about its outcome, one way or the other; God is the judge, and we are the judged, and for us to anticipate the result of the judgment would be to repeat the presumption which brought sin into the world. (Gen. 3:5; see CF VI, 1.)

"the presence of the Lord." Note how this is named as the determining factor of both the bliss of the redeemed and the doom of the damned. If the last judgment has a double issue, as the Confession teaches, there could be no more fitting reward for the righteous than to find Him whom they have sought, and no more fitting punishment for the wicked than eternally to find no end to the quest they have not made (the torments of hell may consist in an "eternal recurrence" or an endless continuation of the status quo). There is, however, another element in the Biblical picture of the consummation, of which the Confession fails to take account. In the Bible the fulfillment of God's purpose of salvation is presented in terms of a redeemed society, the kingdom of God, and not in terms of individuals alone with God, as the Confession tends to do. The presence of others as well as the presence of God will contribute to the bliss of the redeemed.

CF XXXV,3   As Christ would have us to be certainly persuaded that there shall be a day of judgment, both to deter all men from sin, and for the greater consolation of the godly in their adversity: so will he have that day unknown to men, that they may shake off all carnal security, and be always watchful, because they know not at what hour the Lord will come; and may be ever prepared to say, Come, Lord Jesus, come quickly. Amen.

In basing its call for preparedness primarily on the unpredictability of the day of judgment, the Confession, as was said above, fosters the impression that decisive importance attaches to the behavior of men at the moment of its occurrence. This kind of preoccupation with the uncertainty of the date is as likely to generate an attitude of complete unpreparedness ("This year? Next year? Sometime? Never?"—compare II Peter 3:4). The right preparation will surely be based on the certainty of judgment rather than on the uncertainty of the date.